# TY COBB

# TY

## SAFE AT HOME

# COBB

### THE LYONS PRESS

Guilford, Connecticut
*An imprint of The Globe Pequot Press*

## DON RHODES

B
COBB

Copyright © 2008 by Don Rhodes

ALL RIGHTS RESERVED. No part of this book may be reproduced or transmitted in any form by any means, electronic or mechanical, including photocopying and recording, or by any in-formation storage and retrieval system, except as may be expressly permitted in writing from the publisher. Requests for permission should be addressed to The Globe Pequot Press, Attn: Rights and Permissions Department, P.O. Box 480, Guilford, CT 06437.

The Lyons Press is an imprint of The Globe Pequot Press.

Designed by Milly Iacono

Library of Congress Cataloging-in-Publication Data is available on file.

ISBN 978-0-7627-4480-0

Printed in the United States of America

10 9 8 7 6 5 4 3 2 1

Don't ever give up. Don't be a quitter. Play the game to the limit from the time you start up till the last man is called out in the last inning.

Baseball is a funny game, and no game is hopelessly lost until the last man is out. Never hold the ball. Get it back in play as quickly as possible. Fractions of seconds on the ball field are too valuable to be wasted when you are taking part in a play that may save a score.

Be natural, and don't copy. Know your own faults and strive to overcome them.

— Tyrus Raymond Cobb
Quoted by Henry P. Edwards,
Sports Editor, *Cleveland Plain Dealer*, 1922

To my superwise father, Ollen Columbus Rhodes, and his wife of thirty-five years, Jean Swann Rhodes, for their great love of baseball (especially the Atlanta Braves) and their many years of supporting my journalistic endeavors and forgiving my foolishness. It was my dad who paid for most of my college education and gave me the chance to pursue my love of writing, history, and people in general, and for that alone I'll always be grateful. And it was Jean who never has tried to be my stepmother but always tried to be my friend.

# CONTENTS

# Foreword

My first memory of Grandfather Cobb was when he visited us in Daytona Beach, Florida, in 1956. I was eight years old and vaguely knew that he had been a famous baseball player. My older brothers, Ty III and Charlie, were very excited and invited many of their friends to meet him. He attended a Little League game, and I took him to school to meet my class at "show and tell."

The most memorable time was our trip to central Florida to visit (Baseball Hall of Famer) Nap Lajoie. We sat on his porch while they laughed and swapped old baseball stories.

The next year we visited my grandfather's home in Atherton, California. I got him to autograph scraps of paper, which I sold for 50 cents when I returned to Daytona. I still have three!

Visits were infrequent after that.

I last saw him at Emory University Hospital shortly before his death. Mother drove us up to Cornelia, Georgia, from Daytona Beach, for the funeral. I remember very little about the trip except for the long ride from the chapel in Cornelia to the cemetery in Royston. I do recall being amazed by the number of people who lined the road to Royston, hands or hats over their hearts.

As I grew older, I became more aware of what a famous ballplayer my grandfather had been. I made yearly trips to California to visit Grandma

(Charlie) Cobb and my aunts, Shirley Beckworth and Beverly McLaren, and cousins. They gave me many items of grandfather's memorabilia—some of which I have on loan to the Ty Cobb Museum.

Aunt Shirley and Aunt Bev would occasionally share stories about their father, but they never spoke of him in an affectionate manner—perhaps with respect, awe, and even fear—but never affection. My mom rarely talked about Grandfather. We really never discussed him, but I wonder if her indifference resulted from the strained relationship that my father—Ty Cobb Jr.—had with his father. I do know their differences were forgotten by the time of my father's death at age forty-two (in 1952).

I have read many of the books, periodicals, and newspaper accounts of Grandfather, and I have seen the movies, stage plays, and TV documentaries. There is no question that his public image has declined. To examine the character of a famous person is fair. His family, teammates, opponents, and knowledgeable baseball fans past and present would argue that Ty Cobb was a mean, cruel, combative, mostly friendless man.

His legacy? To some the negative aspects will outweigh everything. To others, his baseball records make him the "Greatest Baseball Player Ever."

To me, his legacy is the Ty Cobb Healthcare System in Royston, which began as a hospital he funded and serves northeastern Georgia, and the Ty Cobb Educational Foundation funded by him in 1953. Today that is worth approximately $15 million with around $100,000 in scholarships awarded to Georgia students each year. That's pretty awesome!

And, yes, to me, he also was the greatest baseball player ever.

—Peggy Cobb Schug

# PREFACE

Edward J. Cashin, my friend and chairman of the history and political science department at Augusta (Georgia) State University, first stirred my interest in Tyrus Raymond Cobb with his 1980 book, *The Story of Augusta*. It mentioned that then New Jersey governor Woodrow Wilson, on a visit to his childhood city in November 1911, had seen Augusta resident Ty Cobb act in a play called *The College Widow*.

First of all, I had no idea that Cobb had ever lived in Augusta.

Second of all, as a newspaper writer of entertainment and political stories, I didn't know Cobb had ever acted in a play.

And, third of all, I was intrigued by this unique crossing in history of a future U.S. president and one of the most famous figures in sports.

That interest led to an article I wrote for the afternoon *Augusta Herald* on August 5, 1982, about that meeting between Cobb and Wilson. It prompted a letter from educator Cashin congratulating my research and—much to my pride and pleasure—telling me he had read my article to his history class.

The next month, I expanded my interest of Cobb into a five-part series published September 13–17, in the *Herald*. This time my investigative talents led to lengthy phone conversations with Cobb's two daughters, Beverly

McLaren and Shirley Beckworth, and to a fascinating and emotional trip to Cobb's childhood hometown of Royston, Georgia, culminating with my standing by the mausoleum that contains his earthly remains.

Many good things resulted from that series, with two of the best being the reprinting of my series in the *News Leader* in Royston and a warm letter from Shirley Cobb Beckworth. From her home in Portola Valley, California, Mrs. Beckworth wrote on September 30, 1982:

> *My dear Don Rhodes,*
>
> *Please forgive my tardiness. Blame it all on this third d____ stroke.*
>
> *I received your articles and I must say that errors were too few to mention.*
>
> *Of course, there were some remarks I would rather not have seen, but that's that. I think over all you did an excellent, fair series about a very complex human being.*
>
> *Ford Frick's remark in the last series rather captured T.R.C.[1]*
>
> *What I regretted it was such a lost unhappy life. But maybe that is what he wished. We all walk to a different pace and listen to a different drummer.*
>
> *The scandal which kept him in baseball, as I remember, was about Tris Speaker [manager of Cleveland and Cobb manager of the Detroit Tigers] you mention as 1917 was too early. After all, he played with Connie Mack his last two years and he retired in 1928.*
>
> *Augusta was our home. We went to Detroit when school was out and returned when school began. Augusta was our home. He merely rented in Detroit and Philadelphia.*
>
> *My sister [Beverly] is slightly confused about some items but really nothing important about T.R.C.*

---

1 The quote referred to by Mrs. Beckworth by then Commissioner Frick at the time of Cobb's death was, "We have many baseball players but few Ty Cobbs. He belongs with the [Babe] Ruths, [Christy] Mathewsons, [Grover Cleveland] Alexanders, and [Walter] Johnsons of a golden era."

*Thank you for bringing out some features about T.R.C. that have never been brought forth.*

*I don't believe he missed the cheers and applause [in thirty-three years of retirement before his death in 1961]. He had done that, and that was that.*

*He was a person who found it very difficult to express his deepest feelings and emotions.*

*Hope I've not been too critical.*

*Sincerely,*
*Shirley Beckworth*

*P.S. It might be interesting to note Peggy Schug, out of all his children and grandchildren, is the only one who shares some of his spirit.*

In mid-December 1982, Royston newspaper editor Jeff Frazier sent me some copies of my series as reprinted in the *News Leader* and pleased me greatly by writing, "Again I want to thank you for letting me reprint them. We've received quite a few comments on the series and, as of today, we're close to being sold out at the newstands."

Wow! I was being read by several people who actually had known him!

Seven years later, in June 1989, Mrs. Beckworth again would be writing me, thanking me for copies of old Augusta news stories about her father I had sent her: "You certainly spent a great deal of time researching Cobb. It is too bad others hadn't done more before they wrote their so-called books. My sister went to Yale to see the play [Lee Blessing's play, *Cobb*] and said it was rather awful. It interests me that no one, I mean not one, has ever spoken to me. I'm the oldest living child and know quite a bit.

You know it makes one feel, why strive to reach the top, for it seems then you are attacked, and no one seems to wish to take the time to obtain the truth. Personally, I don't feel anyone can do a biography on him as he was too complex for many to understand."

Probably, Mrs. Beckworth is correct in her belief no one can do Cobb justice. But this is my shot at it, and if I don't hit my mark, at least I have learned an enormous amount in the process about baseball and its players nationwide and particularly in Augusta, Georgia.

It was surprising to me, for instance, to learn Abner Doubleday did not invent the modern game of baseball, as so many believe. In reality a New York bank teller named Alexander Cartwright convinced his ball-playing friends in the spring of 1845 that they should organize some sort of ball club. They called themselves the Knickerbocker Base Ball Club, and they transformed the game from a children's pastime into a sport for adults.[2]

Eventually, forty-six years after his death, the Baseball Hall of Fame in 1938 recognized Cartwright's contributions to the sport by inducting him into the Hall of Fame in an executive category. His unique life also was profiled by New York City librarian Robert Henderson in his 1947 book, *Bat, Ball and Bishop*. The U.S. Congress also offered Cartwright sort of a public apology for overlooking him in June of 1953 by citing Henderson's biography and giving credit to Cartwright for establishing the game of baseball as we know it today.

But, in the major scheme of things, why does it really matter to average baseball fans who actually founded the sport they love so much?

Very simply, it is important to know in any game of life what is the truth and what is not. That's how I personally feel about the life of Tyrus Raymond Cobb.

Cobb's life was lived out on the front pages and sports pages of his local newspapers that covered his fast rise to worldwide fame, his two marriages and his two divorces, his becoming the highest paid player in baseball, his involvement in a 1926 baseball scandal and his subsequent exoneration, his being voted the first player into the Baseball Hall of Fame, his honors and his troubles in retirement, and, of course, his death itself.

Playwrights, movie directors, and authors who have ignored the facts and only want to paint Cobb as a racist, miserly, foul-tempered,

---

2 Cartwright and his friends established three basic concepts still utilized in the game today: They increased the distance between bases to ninety feet, divided the playing area into "fair" and "foul" areas that narrowed the hitting range and reduced the number of defensive players needed, and eliminated the children's way of getting a baseball player "out" by directly throwing the ball at the runner who was trying to play a game of dodge ball rather than "base ball."

lonely old man haven't given fair play to the good times in Tyrus Raymond Cobb's life, when his friends and fans showered him with praise and gifts; when presidents of the United States and captains of American industry loved to golf and hunt with him; when he shared his Augusta home with some of the most famous people of the day; when he spent his off-season days enjoying cars, books, and the theater; and when he took the time to teach many children about the fun and fundamentals of a game that he loved more than life itself.

I'm not his defender. I'm not his promoter. I'm not even his definitive biographer. I think Charles C. Alexander, a professor at Ohio University, came as close to anyone to date in filling that role with his 1984 book, *Ty Cobb*.

What I hope to do with this book is to focus on what Alexander and other authors barely have touched upon, and that is Cobb's rich life in Augusta, Georgia, and his emergence from the centuries-old Southern city to become one of the greatest and most famous players in any sport.

Augusta is where Cobb began his professional playing career; where he lived with his close friends, relatives, and faithful supporters (most of whom have never been before mentioned in any book or article); where he met the woman who would become his wife; and where four of his five children would be born.

Cobb did play a rough game of baseball and could be physically cruel in his pursuit of victory. Yes, Cobb was also tight with a buck and equally tight with a penny, but he also gave away thousands of dollars to help good causes and those who had fallen on tough times, including widows of former ballplayers. And, Cobb most likely was a racist, but so were the majority of the other Southerners in Cobb's lifetime (1886–1961).

Yes, Cobb undoubtedly did beat his wife and kids—his kids told me that personally—but they still defended him because he knew that his children would be the subject of intense public scrutiny. He wouldn't have won any "Father of the Year" titles, but Cobb apparently did what he personally thought was best in disciplining his children, and he sent them to the finest schools.

And yes, in his final years, he was a lonely old man who often said and did mean things, partly because of the pain that racked his body, partly because his actions brought him attention, and partly because it was his way of saying that nobody was going to push Ty Cobb around—no umpire, no player, no politician, no powerful businessman, nobody.

I hope, when you finish this book, you will come to the same conclusion that his oldest daughter, Shirley, did in describing her father to me in that 1982 letter as "a very complex human being."

—Don Rhodes
Augusta, Georgia
Home of Ty Cobb

# Acknowledgments

First of all, thanks to my life partner and closest friend, Ervin Edward "Eddie" Smith Jr., for tramping through countless cemeteries with me and letting me take over the dining room table for this book even though he kept asking why I was writing about this dead guy and when was I going to get off "that damn computer."

And to the great four-legged friends and confidants in my life: Fluffy, Little Bit, Wolfie, Foxie, Reba, Toughy, Jasper, Rusty, Will, and Jayme Brown, who have brought me up when two-legged folks took me down.

And, in no particular order, my gratefulness also goes out to the following:

My lunch buddies Duncan Wheale, Russ Mobley, and Pat Claiborne, who enthusiastically encouraged my research, who listened to my latest Cobb trivia discovery without acting too bored, and who asked some pretty good questions that prompted further research.

My sisters Linda Groover, Jan Harris, and Ann Holland; my brothers, Larry Rhodes, Mike Spence, and Doug Spence and their families for caring about me even when they suspect I'm crazy; and to my late mother, Ella Sampert Rhodes, who taught me how to spell (something I'm still learning) and who gave me my love of reading and music. I'll especially remember the great "Cobb Tour" my sister, Linda, and my dad took one day in early

October to relive special moments of Cobb's northern Georgia life in Cornelia, the Narrows community, Carnesville, and Royston.

The Cobb family for trusting me and letting me know the true stories, especially Ty and Charlie Cobb's children: Shirley Cobb Beckworth, Beverly Cobb McLaren, and Jimmy Cobb; their granddaughters Peggy Cobb Schug, Leslie Cameron McLaren, and Shirley McLaren Fisher and their grandson, Charlie Cobb; and also to Ty Cobb's daughters-in-law, Shirley Cobb (Jimmy's wife) and Mary Dunn Cobb (Ty Jr.'s wife). I owe a special debt to Peggy Schug for not only being such a good friend over many years but also for agreeing to write the foreword for this biography of her grandfather. I owe another special debt to Margaret Holley, not only for her close friendship of forty-seven years with Ty Cobb's niece and fellow baseball fan, Elna Anne Lombard, but also for allowing me to visit The Oaks (Charlie Lombard Cobb's home place) and for letting me dig through some dusty boxes of Lombard family photos. Also thanks to Alva Sherman and Beverly Ford for letting me go through the Cobb family house in Augusta that had become their home.

At Morris Communications Company, my coworkers (past and present) in the Morris corporate communications department, Jeff Barnes, John "Bo" Roberts, Leeann Huston, Belinda Thomas, Kay Pruitt, Todd Beasley, Mark Albertin, Paula Scott, Melissa Marcotte, Chris Bender, Cathy Martindale, and Pete May for making it a joy to go to work (most days at least).

Also at Morris Communications, to Billy Morris and his wonderful wife, Sissie; sons, Will and Tyler; and daughter, Susie, for their longtime support of my creative efforts both in and out of the office that hopefully reflect honor back on their great, international, multimedia company, based on Broad Street in Augusta, Georgia.

And to Don Bailey, president of the *Augusta Chronicle*, and executive editor Dennis Sodomka for allowing me extensive usage of the *Chronicle*'s photo and news files, including the incredible augustaarchives.com electronic search tool that allows Ty Cobb fans to read the articles in the *Chronicle* just as Cobb himself did.

Also at the *Chronicle*, special thanks to Sean Moores, Tami Roose, and Rhonda Hollimon for their generous assistance, and to David Playford and

John Barnes of the *Augusta Herald* for allowing me to pursue the Cobb legend in the first place.

Also to the good folks in Royston and Cornelia, Georgia, for their personal memories and assistance, especially Pope Welborn and Susie Bond.

Especially to the many researchers, historians, and Cobb enthusiasts who generously shared their wealth of knowledge, historical materials, and opinions, especially Richard Corley, Ed Sweeny, James Kossuth, Kirk Miner, Joseph M. Lee III, Milledge Murray, Davenport "Dee" Bruker, Bill Baab, Johnny Edwards, Jimmy Lanier, Michael Bishop, William C. Calhoun, Lou Brissie, Linda and Bill Macky, Bill Kirby, Keith Claussen, Paul Hemphill; also Nancy Glaser and Guy Robbins at the Augusta Museum of History; Ed Cashin, John J. O'Shea, and Carol Waggoner-Angleton at Augusta State University; Jerry Murphy at Magnolia Cemetery; Carrie Adamson at the Augusta Genealogy Society; Erick D. Montgomery at the Richmond County Historical Society; Robin L. McLaughlin for her help researching the Cobb graves in Palo Alto, California; Joyce Baskins at the Franklin County Courthouse; Betty Thomas, Kathy Hill, and Vicki Dalton at the Banks County Courthouse; Lloyd Creech, who sent me a postcard of Tigers Stadium from Detroit; Wesley Fricks and William "Bill" Burgess (baseballguru.com) for their e-mails and excellent articles on the baseball-fever.com site; and photographers Frank Christian and Kirk Baxley.

And to my new best friends at Globe Pequot Press in Guilford, Connecticut, including Scott Watrous, Kathryn Mennone, Christine Etlinger, Eugene Brissie, Josh Rosenberg, Mary Norris and, most especially, baseball fan Erin Turner, who not only managed to skillfully and lovingly edit this book from her office and home in Montana but also give birth to her daughter, Stella Jane, during the process.

Finally, thanks to Ty Cobb and his Augusta-born wife, Charlie Lombard Cobb, for being two of the most interesting subjects I've ever come across in my forty-plus years of published writing. I really wish that I had known them both face-to-face during their lifetimes. There are so many more questions I'd love to ask.

# A Brief Chronology of
# the Life of Tyrus Raymond Cobb

*February 23, 1863,* Ty Cobb's father, William Herschel Cobb, is born.

*January 15, 1871,* Ty Cobb's mother, Amanda Chitwood, is born.

*February 11, 1886,* William Herschel Cobb, a rural schoolteacher, marries Amanda Chitwood in Banks County, Georgia. He is twenty-three. She is fifteen.

*December 18, 1886,* Tyrus Raymond Cobb is born in Banks County, Georgia, on his mother's parents' farm in the Narrows community near Cornelia.

*February 23, 1889,* Cobb's brother, John Paul, is born.

*July 3, 1890,* Cobb's future wife, Charlie Marion Lombard, is born in Richmond County, Georgia.

*October 29, 1892,* Cobb's sister, Florence Leslie, is born.

*November 24, 1903,* The South Atlantic Baseball League—later known as the SALLY League—is organized in Savannah with William Henry Sherman representing Augusta.

H. H. Cabaniss, business manager and part owner of the *Augusta Chronicle*, steps up to form a stock company to finance the Augusta team.

*January 1, 1904,* Con Strouthers arrives in Augusta to become the Augusta Tourists first manager and later part owner.

*April 26, 1904,* Cobb plays in his first professional baseball game at Warren Park with the Augusta Tourists playing the Columbia (SC) Skyscrapers.

*April 27, 1904,* after his second game with the Tourists, manager Strouthers drops Cobb from the roster, and Cobb goes with Fred Hays to play for the Anniston (Alabama) Steelers team.

*July 25, 1904,* Augusta Tourists new owner and manager Harlan W. (Harry) Wingard sends Cobb a telegram ordering him "to join the team at once" in Augusta.

*August 9, 1904,* Cobb rejoins the Tourists playing a doubleheader against the Columbia Skycrapers at Warren Park with the first game starting at 3:00 p.m.

*January 29, 1905,* the *Chronicle* reports that Tourists Club president John B. Carter and manager Andy Roth have signed eighteen men to a new contract, of which fourteen would be kept for the new season, including Ty Cobb.

*March 7, 1905,* The Detroit Tigers, led by manager Bill Armour, arrive in Augusta for spring training, giving Armour a close-up look at Cobb's playing skills.

*March 28, 1905,* Augusta Tourists minor league team surprisingly beat Detroit Tigers major-league team at Augusta's Warren Park, 8–7, with Cobb playing for the Tourists against the team he would be playing for by the end of the year.

*August 8, 1905,* Cobb's mother shoots his forty-two-year-old father to death thinking he is a prowler. She contends it is accidental but will be put on trial for murder.

*August 19, 1905,* Augusta Tourists president C. D. Carr confirms reports outfielder Tyrus Cobb has been sold to the Detroit Tigers of the American League for $500.

*August 25, 1905,* Cobb plays his last game with Augusta Tourists as a member of the team. He will join the Tourists for spring practice games several times in later years.

*August 30, 1905,* Cobb makes his debut with the Detroit Tigers.

*March 31, 1906,* Amanda Chitwood Cobb is found not guilty of deliberately killing her husband. She immediately returns to her home in Royston.

*August 6, 1908,* Tyrus Raymond Cobb marries Charlie Marion Lombard at "The Oaks," the Victorian mansion home of her parents, Roswell and Nancy Lombard, in rural Richmond County, nine miles from downtown Augusta. He is twenty-one. She is eighteen.

*January 30, 1910,* Ty and Charlie's first child, Tyrus Raymond Cobb Jr., is born in Augusta.

*October 9, 1910,* Cobb sits out the final day of season to keep his lead in the American League's batting average race over Nap Lajoie, who almost beats him.

*June 2, 1911,* Ty and Charlie's first daughter, Shirley Marion Cobb, is born in Detroit.

*July 4, 1911,* Chicago White Sox pitcher Ed Walsh stops Cobb's forty-game hitting streak.

*October 11, 1911,* Cobb wins the first Most Valuable Player award for the American League.

*November 18, 1911,* Former Augusta resident Woodrow Wilson, then governor of New Jersey and future U.S. president, sees Cobb act as a football hero in the comedy, *The College Widow*, in Augusta's Grand Opera House.

*May 15, 1912,* Cobb takes insults from Claude Lueker, a New York Highlanders fan, until he finally charges into the stands and beats the man. Lueker, it turns out, had lost a hand in an industrial accident and could not defend himself. Ban Johnson, president of the American League, suspends Cobb immediately. The Detroit Tigers subsequently stage a strike in support of Cobb. Other players and managers also contend something needs to be done about fans unreasonably insulting players.

*March 24, 1913,* an Augusta team of players rounded up by Cobb plays the Brooklyn Superbas (later known as the Dodgers) at Warren Park in Augusta. The next day several of the Brooklyn players including Casey Stengel take up a challenge to play basketball against the local YMCA team with the YMCA team winning.

*1916,* Cobb becomes first athlete to star in a commercial motion picture. The movie, *Somewhere in Georgia,* is filmed in New York.

*September 29, 1917,* Ty and Charlie's second son, Roswell Herschel Cobb, is born in Augusta.

*September 30, 1918,* Cobb says good-bye to friends before catching the afternoon train for Washington, D.C., to report for military service as a captain in the army's chemical warfare division.

*December 18, 1918,* Cobb, after service in France, is back in Augusta on his thirty-second birthday.

*April 8, 1919,* Cobb leaves Augusta to join the Detroit Tigers in Columbia, South Carolina, en route to Rock Hill, South Carolina, for an exhibition game against a team from Boston.

*September 19, 1919,* Ty and Charlie's second daughter, Beverly Cobb, is born in Augusta.

*December 18, 1920,* Detroit Tigers president/owner Frank J. Navin announces the Georgia Peach will be the manager of the Tigers for the 1921 season.

*February 1, 1921,* Cobb is honored at a banquet in Detroit in recognition of his becoming the Tigers new manager.

*July 24, 1921,* Ty and Charlie's last child and third son, James Howell Cobb, is born in Augusta.

*August 19, 1921,* Cobb makes his 3,000th hit.

*May 5, 1925,* Cobb has the best game in his career while playing against the St. Louis Browns in St. Louis. He hits 3 home runs, 1 double, and 2 singles. The next day he hits 2 more home runs.

*August 29, 1925,* Detroit fans of Cobb host a huge banquet in honor of Cobb's twentieth anniversary playing for the Tigers.

*November 3, 1926,* Cobb confirms an announcement by Detroit Tigers owner Frank Navin that Cobb has resigned as manager and player with the Tigers and is quitting baseball.

*November 29, 1926,* Tris Speaker resigns as player and manager of the Cleveland Indians.

*December 21, 1926,* Three days after Cobb's fortieth birthday, the *Augusta Herald* reports Cobb and Speaker are being investigated for an "alleged irregularity" involving a game played in Detroit between the Tigers and the Cleveland Indians on September 25, 1919.

*January 27, 1927,* Commissioner Landis clears Cobb and Speaker of any impropriety and orders them reinstated by their clubs.

*February 8, 1927,* Cobb accepts an offer to play for Connie Mack's Philadelphia Athletics at the then staggering salary of $60,000 per year.

*July 18, 1927,* As a member of the Athletics, Cobb gets his 4,000th career hit with a double in the first inning, while playing against the Detroit Tigers.

*May 24, 1928,* Cobb plays in a game between the Philadelphia Athletics and the New York Yankees. The game features thirteen future members of the Baseball Hall of Fame including Cobb.

*June 15, 1928,* Cobb steals home plate for his fifty-fourth and final time.

*September 11, 1928,* Cobb plays his final game of professional baseball on the home turf of the New York Yankees before 40,000 fans with the Yankees, led by George Herman "Babe" Ruth, beating the Athletics, 5–3.

*April 24, 1930,* Cobb is in Columbia, South Carolina, for both the opening of the new Columbia airport and to toss out the first ball opening the 1930 season of the South Atlantic League.

*April 16, 1931,* the *Augusta Chronicle* reports Cobb's wife has sued for a divorce. Cobb is in California attending the opening of the San Francisco baseball club's new Seal Stadium when informed of the news. The Cobbs later patch up their problems, and the family moves to California.

*February 2, 1936,* The first inductees into the Baseball Hall of Fame are named in Cooperstown, New York, with Cobb leading the number of ballots cast to become the first player voted into the hall. Others inducted that first year are Babe Ruth, Honus Wagner, Christy Mathewson, and Walter Johnson.

*March 14, 1947,* High-power attorney Melvin Belli tells reporters he expects Charlie Cobb to reach an out-of-court settlement in her suit for a division of community property that she sets at $7 million. The next day, however, Charlie withdraws her suit giving no reason for her change of mind.

*June 19, 1947,* Judge William McKnight in Reno, Nevada, announces he has granted a decree of divorce to Cobb on the grounds that he and his wife had been separated for at least three years.

*March 26, 1949,* Cobb is back in Royston for the groundbreaking of a hospital dedicated to the memory of his parents. He had given $100,000 the previous October for the funding of the hospital whose total cost of $250,000 would be made up of Cobb's gift and federal funds. It will develop into a major health-care system serving residents of several North Georgia counties. Cobb called the groundbreaking "the happiest day of my life."

*September 24, 1949,* Cobb marries Frances Fairbairn Cass on September 24, 1949, in Buffalo, New York. He is sixty-two. She is thirty-nine.

*April 13, 1951,* Roswell Herschel Cobb becomes the first of Ty and Charlie's five children to die with his death coming in San Louis Obispo, California, from a heart attack at the age of thirty-three.

*September 9, 1952,* Tyrus Raymond Cobb Jr. dies in Woodside, California, of a brain tumor at the age of forty-two.

*January 28, 1954,* Cobb and his wife, Frances, meet with FBI director J. Edgar Hoover at the FBI headquarters in Washington, D.C., and were given a special tour including the exhibit rooms, the FBI laboratory, the Diorama, and the indoor firing range. Cobb earlier had offered to supply the FBI with any information he might obtain about organized crime trying to infiltrate professional baseball. He had stated, however, "he could not see how organized baseball as such could be of any value whatsoever to any subversive organization."

*September 7, 1955,* the second Mrs. Cobb files for divorce.

*August 27, 1957,* Cobb is honored in Augusta for the third and last time with the occasion being Ty Cobb Day at Jennings Stadium in Allen Park off Walton Way.

*April 27, 1961,* Cobb attends his last baseball game at Wrigley Field in Los Angeles, California, and throws out the first ball, with the Los Angeles Angels playing the Minnesota Twins.

*July 17, 1961,* Cobb dies from complications of diabetes and cancer in Emory University Hospital in an Atlanta suburb at age seventy-four with his first wife, Charlie, by his side. She never remarried.

*July 18, 1961,* Cobb's funeral is held in the chapel of McGahee Funeral Home in Cornelia, Georgia, with the honorary pallbearers being members of the Ty Cobb Educational Foundation and the staff of Ty Cobb Memorial Hospital. His body is transported to the mausoleum in Royston that he built for his mother, father, sister, and himself.

*February 24, 1975,* Charlie Marion Lombard Cobb dies in Portola Valley, California, at eighty-four.

# TOURISTS GIVE COBB A CHANCE      1

IF YOU STAND BY THE GRAVE of Confederate army captain William Henry War-ren in tree-shaded Magnolia Cemetery in Augusta, Georgia, and look past the old brick wall and just across Third Street, you can see the Exchange Club of Augusta's fairgrounds. The eastern side of the fairgrounds, just a ball's throw away, once was a baseball field called Warren Park, and it was at Warren Park on Memorial Day, April 26, 1904, that sports history was made when seventeen-year-old Tyrus Raymond Cobb played his first professional game of baseball.

The newly formed Augusta Tourists team were part of the also newly formed South Atlantic League (commonly referred to as the SALLY League) created in late November of 1903, with Augusta joining five other Southern cities: Jacksonville, Florida; Savannah and Macon, Georgia; and Columbia and Charleston, South Carolina.

On January 2, 1904, the *Augusta Chronicle* announced that Con Strouthers, the new and first manager of Augusta's club in the South Atlantic League, had arrived in the city on the first day of the new year. The *Chronicle* reported that "Mr. Strouthers will not only manage and play first base but will operate the club himself." Strouthers, in fact, had become owner of the Augusta club franchise.[1]

---

1 Strouthers played for St. Louis in 1896 and then went to the Pacific Slope. His next job was as manager of the team in Omaha, Nebraska, before moving to the Southern League, where he became manager of the teams in Birmingham, Alabama, and Chattanooga, Tennessee. Strouthers had started his career as a team manager in 1894 for the Kansas City, Kansas, team. The next year found him as manager and player for the Detroit club. His last engagement in the South before Augusta was in Chattanooga two years earlier.

"This gentleman comes highly recommended as a player and a man of business methods," the *Chronicle* continued. "He has the looks, manners and speech of a young collegian and gives every evidence of being first class in every respect. He, like a number of young men in the North and West, has entered baseball as a business career. He runs a team like a man would a factory or a store. To him, it is no pastime, but a business profession. He understands thoroughly that he has to please his patrons and that the only way to accomplish this task is to have a good team."

Strouthers had been in the city only one day when he told the *Chronicle*, "I have been all over Augusta today, looked at the people, their dress, their homes and, in fact, everything that would serve as an indication to a stranger and if Augusta is not a good town I am very much mistaken."

The obvious location for the needed ballpark and home base for the new Augusta team naturally was a large area already being used for baseball games at the turn of the twentieth century. It was bounded on the east by Third Street, on the west by Fourth, on the south by Hale Street, and on the north by Walton Way.[2]

The *Chronicle* would report, "The season will open April 26, Memorial Day, in the three Georgia cities: Charleston will play in Savannah, Jacksonville in Macon and Columbia in Augusta. The day is a holiday in all of the Georgia cities, and as Memorial Day is not observed until later in the summer in the other towns of the league. It was decided that the best idea was to follow that arrangement.

"No double headers will be played until after July," the article continued, "and one ladies day will be observed in all cities of the league. On that day the ladies will be admitted to the grounds and grandstand free of charge."

The *Chronicle* put in its two cents in noting, "Perhaps, the best name yet suggested is the Tourists, in deference to Augusta's fame as a winter resort."

Sure enough, Augustans woke up on the morning of April 10, 1904, to read an informative *Chronicle* headline proclaiming: AUGUSTA'S TEAM TO BE NAMED TOURISTS.

---

2 Today, if you face the Hale Street gate of the Exchange Club of Augusta fairgrounds, the ball-playing field that was Warren Park is to your left with the covered grandstand pretty much right in front of you. There are concrete-block bathrooms to your far left at the southeast corner of Third and Hale Streets where once existed dressing rooms for the players.

"It is the 'Tourists,'" the newspaper said. "Manager Con Strouthers definitely decided upon this name yesterday for the Augusta ball team. This is the name that was given to the team two weeks or more ago by the *Chronicle* and used constantly since in referring to the organization."

To those who know of the role of Augusta on the Georgia side of the Savannah River and of North Augusta and Aiken on the South Carolina side as winter colonies for the very rich families of the north in pre-Florida days, it was a good and natural choice.[3]

The same article in which Strouthers announced the Tourists would be the name of the Augusta ball club also revealed, "The ball grounds have been named Warren Park after the late lamented Captain W. H. Warren. This is an appropriate name and will unquestionably be a go with the fans of the city."[4]

The *Chronicle* article telling of the team's new name and the name of the renovated Augusta playing field also revealed how much the Augusta team management regarded the role advertising could play in the success of the new professional athletic venture, which seems impressive for 1904.

"Yesterday Manager Strouthers received the lithograph poster and window placards which will be used in advertising the games during the season. The big posters, the same as those used by shows for bill boards, are beauties and will attract general attention. They represent a ball game

---

3 Manager Strouthers said the worst name submitted—and most agree he was right—was the Grave Diggers, apparently in reference to Magnolia Cemetery being across Third Street from the baseball park.

4 Capt. William Henry Warren had died a few months earlier about 5:00 p.m. on October 14, 1903. Although Warren was born in Cayuga County, New York, he had moved in his early youth to Nashville, Tennessee, and when the Civil War came along, he volunteered with the Rock City Guards. Once the war was over, Warren decided to stay in Augusta. He married the daughter of prominent local landowner N. B. Moore and devoted himself to the management of the well-known Moore Farm, which consisted of more than one hundred acres just beyond the eastern boundary of the city. He became an expert in agricultural methods, especially haymaking. He became president of the Richmond Agricultural Society and was appointed in 1892 to the board of directors of the Georgia Experiment Station. He also became an elder in Augusta's First Presbyterian Church and president of the YMCA, which gave him the opportunity to work with the athletic development of Augusta's young men. Warren's good friend, Prosper J. Berckmans, whose nursery (Fruitland) would become the grounds of the Augusta National Golf Club, said of Warren, "He took an especial interest in the welfare of young men as well as whatever concerned public and civic improvements, to which he was ever ready to extend generous aid. Benevolent with discrimination and unostentatious in manner, he knew how to give well, thus proving himself a true philanthropist and consistent Christian."

at a critical stage when a batter has hit the ball and it is a close race to beat the ball out to first base. The umpire is close at hand and using his peepers for all they are worth.

"The show window advertisements are also very pretty, giving a baseball scene and bear the date of the opening game in Augusta, and the entire home schedule of the Augusta team.

"This mode of advertising will be used in all of the smaller towns contingent to Augusta, and it is believed to advantage. Aiken, Waynesboro, Langley and Graniteville have a number of great fans and it is the attention of the local management to get them interested in the Augusta aggregation."

Little by little, baseball fans began learning more and more about what to expect on opening day: a flag with the name "Warren Park" to be placed on top of the grandstand; new bleachers seating an additional 500 just ten feet to the right of the grandstand, bringing the total available seats to about 2,500; and a "neat fence" built to separate the area reserved for spectators "from the territory of the players."

There also was a bench near the scoreboard with a top to keep the sun off provided for the visiting team, and a top for the home players bench, which was situated under the grandstand.

As the behind-the-scenes particulars fell into place, the players themselves started arriving.

In all likelihood, Tyrus Raymond Cobb probably found out about the Southern League from his father's newspaper, the *Royston Record*, or another local newspaper telling about the new baseball organization and teams just a few hours south of Royston. The story that Cobb himself told several times is that he wrote letters to all six of the SALLY league teams seeking a position, but only one team replied: the Augusta Tourists.

Cobb said he was offered a contract of $50 per month but was told he would have to pay his own way to Augusta and was responsible for his living expenses.

Cobb also would contend that even though his father wanted him to attend a Georgia university, he still sat down and wrote six checks of $15 each to help his son make his baseball dreams come true.

(Susie Bond of Royston, whose father was Joe T. Cunningham, one of Cobb's closest boyhood friends, told this author it was really Cobb's mother's brother-in-law, Clifford A. Ginn, who paid for Cobb's train trip to Augusta. Mrs. Bond's father and Ginn were about four years older than Cobb but all three played together on the Royston Reds baseball team.)

On Saturday, April 9, 1904, the *Augusta Chronicle* in one brief paragraph wrote an entirely new page in baseball history in telling its readers, "The players that have reported are as follows: Catcher Dave Edmonds, Shortstop Young, Pitcher Durham, Fielder McMillin, Infielder Thornton, Fielder Cobb, Pitcher Brown."

In the days leading up to the April 26 season opener, the *Chronicle* mentioned Cobb several times and gave him the nickname "Sleuth" (before he was nicknamed "The Georgia Peach"): "Cobb is still running loose in left field. He gets everything in sight and is a natural hitter. There is no drawing away from the base with him, but he wades right into 'em and clouts 'em out."

"Cobb made several good catches of long drives in the field yesterday."

"McMillin gave Cobb quite a scare Thursday. Thornton, Cobb and Mc-Millen were passing 'em around when Cobb threw Mac a floater and after he did this he executed a war dance. Mac seeing that the young fellow was not looking yelled out 'Back to the plow for you, Sleuth!' 'Sleuth,' hearing the bark thought somebody had thrown a ball at him, and the way he was dodging was real exhilarating."

"Cobb made a good catch of Edmonds' line hit in right field yesterday. It looked good for a couple, but 'Sleuth' got under and copped it."

"Cobb has a bat that has spring in it. It is spliced and when it hits the ball rebounds several inches. It is called the 'Biffer.' Go down and watch him biff 'em around the diamond."

"Cobb slid in home yesterday and one could hear his body grating against the ground. He came up all right, but out."

"Cobb, utility man, a youngster, is a great hitter and fast in the field. Will make a big leaguer in a year or two."

In spite of the positive preseason buzz, Memorial Day of April 26, 1904, started out very dreary for the managers and players of the Augusta Tourists and Columbia Skyscrapers baseball clubs as they woke up in their Augusta hotels. Steady rain was falling at dawn that Tuesday and kept coming down intermittently until about 11:00 a.m. when the sun finally came out. That afternoon, they would be facing each other for the first time in the just-formed South Atlantic League. Game time at Warren Park was set for 3:30 p.m.

"At two o'clock the two teams headed by the Sacred Heart Cadets Band took a ride around the belt line, attracting considerable attention and creating great enthusiasm along their course," the *Chronicle* related the next day. "The two teams were in full uniform and looked every inch ball players."

The threat of rain didn't keep the fans away, and an estimated 2,000 fans had packed the grandstand and two bleachers when the game was called at 3:45 p.m. Part of that excellent, first-day turnout for a city Augusta's size was due to a Mexican music teacher, Señor Jose Andonegui, who had organized the Augusta Rooters Club.[5] "The Rooters will devote each afternoon to rooting at the ball park," the *Chronicle* said of the organization that undoubtedly became the first fan support group in Augusta and may have been one of the first in the South. "They are not knockers but rooters. They propose to make it a hard road for all opponents of the Augusta club to travel. They are going to help the Tourists win games."

For that first Augusta Tourists game, Cobb was not even in the announced lineup printed in that morning's edition of the *Chronicle*. Printed the morning of April 26, the lineup was as follows:

- ◆ Spratt, *third base*
- ◆ Butler, *center field*
- ◆ McMillin, *left field*
- ◆ Truby, *second base*
- ◆ Bussey, *first base*
- ◆ Edmonds, *right field*
- ◆ Roth, *catcher*
- ◆ Thornton, *shortstop*
- ◆ Durham, *pitcher*

---

5 When Andonegui returned from a European trip in August of 1909, he told the *Chronicle* that people on the other side of the Atlantic Ocean know little of baseball, "but they have all heard of Ty Cobb and know he is in the game."

In later years, Cobb recalled that Harry Bussey was forced out of that first game due to his being contractually obligated to playing for another team. But just prior to the game on April 26, it was catcher Andy Roth who was ordered out of the game by John H. Farrell, secretary-treasurer of the National Association of Professional Baseball Leagues, due to Roth being contractually obligated to playing for a team in Nashville, Tennessee. The next day, the *Chronicle* published the opening day's roster that reflected Roth's situation:

- Spratt, *third base*
- Butler, *right field*
- McMillin, *left field*
- Truby, *second base*
- Bussey, *first base*
- Edmonds, *catcher*
- Cobb, *center field*
- Thornton, *shortstop*
- Durham, *pitcher*

Manager Strouthers wound up switching rightfielder Dave Edmonds to catcher, moving the centerfielder to right field, and, in a history-making move, substituting Cobb for Butler in center field. The contract problems with Roth were quickly resolved, and he was in the Tourists lineup for the next day's game against Columbia at Warren Park. Cobb was listed in the *Chronicle* as again playing center field in that game.

But when the Augusta team played the Columbia team in Columbia on April 28 and April 29, Cobb was not a part of the Tourists lineup. Butler had been moved from playing left field to Cobb's position as centerfielder. McMillin, who had played left field in the Tourists first game in Augusta, had been moved to Butler's position in left field.

Cobb had been dropped mysteriously from the roster by manager Strouthers and soon afterward joined the Anniston (Alabama) Steelers team of the Southeastern League, where another Tourist player, Fred Hays, had recently gone. "Young and Brown are still in the city," the *Chronicle* briefly reported on May 2, 1904. "Cobb and Hays left for Anniston several days ago where they will play with that team."

Cobb being dropped from the Tourists especially was surprising since the *Chronicle* had high praise for Cobb in his professional game debut in which he had a double in the eighth inning and a home run in the ninth. Writing about the top of the ninth inning, with the Tourists fighting to win their first game, the *Chronicle* noted, "Cobb, the first man up, slammed the ball over the ridge in left field for a clean home run. The grandstand and bleachers went wild with delight."

Even though the effort failed to win the game, the Tourists losing by one run, 8–7, the newspaper was still happy with the team's effort, writing the next day, "While the crowd was disappointed in that Augusta did not win, the game was exciting and interesting from start to finish. . . . It was a game in which the spectators got their money's worth, full measure, running over. Columbia deserved the victory."

The *Chronicle* had several other glowing comments about Cobb's performance in that first SALLY League game:

"Cobb's two-bagger in the eighth inning started the ball rolling and almost won the game," the *Chronicle* wrote on April 27 following the Tourists loss. "His home run was a peacherina. He is going to make a good man."

"Cobb, the boy from Royston. Royston bids fair to become as well known as Jasper, where Henley came from. Who knows where Royston is? Look it up on a map."

"Cobb's black bat did it. He has been saving that bat for two weeks for just such an occasion. Maybe the fans didn't cheer him when he came to the plate after he knocked the two-bagger, but when he knocked the home run everybody went bughouse."

"Cobb has only to keep up the gait he has struck to land a berth on the team. His work yesterday stamped him as a comer."

In later years the manager gave his reason for dropping Cobb: Strouthers would not work with anyone who would not take orders. That could be true because the *Chronicle*, in a profile of Cobb on October 19, 1913, wrote, "And it was in Augusta that he was ordered to 'bunt' with two men on bases when the game was hanging in the balance and was 'fired' for knocking the cover off the ball and making a home run. From this incident, Ty Cobb dated as a great ball player."

But another clue as to what might have happened between Strouthers and Cobb came with a brief *Chronicle* notice on May 1, 1904, a few days after Cobb had left the team, saying, "Strouthers, in his anxiety to help the boys along, coached from the bench and was put out of the grounds."

Strouthers had a temper.

Three months after Cobb was fired from the Tourists, Strouthers sold his ownership in the Augusta Tourists and left Augusta. On July 20, 1904, the *Chronicle* announced that H. W. Wingard and a group of investors had purchased the team. Wingard would be the manager. The article continued, "This announcement will be received with pleasure throughout the city. It means that the Augusta franchise in the South Atlantic league has passed into the hands of local gentlemen in whom the ball public will have confidence, free of any taint of jockeyism or queering."

The new owner—and manager—Harlan (Harry) W. Wingard obviously had been thinking of good ways to improve the team and attendance at games. As the *Chronicle* reported: "Manager Wingard also promises to pay strict attention to the details of the sport with an idea of popularizing it with the best people of the city. He announces that hereafter every Thursday will be ladies' day. That means that they will be passed free of charge both at the gate and grandstand. On other days the usual price at the gate will be charged. The refreshment stand will also be reopened and run strictly up to date."

Wingard additionally told the *Chronicle*, "As I discover the weak places in the team, I shall make an honest effort to strengthen. It will be no bluff game with me. I am here to stay this season and also next. I could not expect the patronage of the public unless I treat them on the square."

One of the first things Wingard did to "strengthen" the Tourists was to get Cobb back on the team. On July 26, 1904, the *Chronicle* told Tourists fans, "Manager Wingard is confident that he will have several new faces on the team by the opening of the next Augusta series. Last night he wired Fielder Cobb to join the team at once. A letter was received from Cobb expressing a willingness to report if needed. He explained that Manager

Strouthers during his administration tried several times to get him to return to the team, but that he did not care to play under his administration."

Once Strouthers was gone from the Augusta team and Wingard was running the show, Cobb was ready to return to Augusta and give the Tourists another try. That decision would change his life and the game of baseball forever.

The next day, on Tuesday, July 27, the *Chronicle* reported, "Fielder Stickney, because of his inability to connect with the ball except at rare intervals, was canned Monday night. He will be succeeded by Cobb who wires that he will join the team in time for this afternoon's game if it is possible to do so. With Cobb in the game, the Tourists will have a hitting and fielding team in the outer gardens second to none in the league. They are Kennedy, Engel and Cobb."

On August 9, 1904, Cobb was back with the Tourists at Warren Park against the Columbia Skycrapers. Cobb had a miserable day as centerfielder. He came to bat four times but did not get a single base hit. The Tourists lost to Columbia, 4–2, with rain cutting short the final inning.

Cobb had a better showing against Columbia the next day scoring one of Augusta's three runs in a game that ended tied at 3 after ten innings. Cobb bunted in the sixth inning and got to first base when the pitcher fumbled and then he stole second. He sprinted for home when Clyde Engle got a single.

There was no Hollywood ending after Cobb rejoined the Tourists that year. It was a rather sad mid-September finish for the Tourists that first season in spite of Wingard taking control and Cobb returning to the team. The team finished last in the SALLY League that inaugural season, with the team from Macon, Georgia, taking the league's pennant.

Even with Cobb back on the roster and with all his good intentions, Wingard couldn't turn the team around. The team was in a financial crisis and Wingard was unable to pay the players in early August of 1904. Several prominent Augustans talked it over and came to the conclusion that if they didn't help Wingard out, the franchise might be lost and there might be no chance of locals being in charge of the team the next year. So, they loaned Wingard $1,000. The players reported receiving $20 each and being assured they would get the rest of their salary later.

By December 1904, Wingard had sold his interest in the Augusta Tourists and given up his manager role. Catcher Andy Roth was made the acting manager. His arrival on the team in early 1904 had been eagerly anticipated by Augusta fans. "Andy has a throw that starts the ball away without any jerk to the arm," the *Chronicle* had reported the day after he got in town, "but it travels like a bullet. He has a good swing throw to third, which is great for catching a runner when a man is on third and one on first. Andy says, 'When a man's on third and one's on first and he tries to steal, well, that's my morning star.'"

It would be the new acting manager Roth and Augusta Tourists Baseball Club president John B. Carter who would make the decision to keep Cobb on the team for the 1905 season.

While baseball fans can thank the Tourists first manager Con Strouthers for hiring Cobb and putting the north Georgia youngster in his first professional game, they also can blame him for almost letting Cobb slip away from baseball history after only two games.

Harlan (Harry) W. Wingard—almost never mentioned in Cobb biographies or baseball history books—brought Cobb back to Augusta and put him on the right track to sports immortality. And yet when Wingard died on March 8, 1962, in New Orleans, Louisiana, "after an extended illness," just the year after Cobb died in Georgia, the *Chronicle* only devoted two paragraphs to his passing and never once mentioned his role in the saga of Ty Cobb.

For many baseball historians, the legend of Ty Cobb began in Detroit on August 30, 1905. But for those who know the real story, the legend really began with Cobb's first professional game at Augusta's Warren Park more than one hundred years ago, on April 26, 1904.

# BECOMING A MAJOR LEAGUER                    2

ON JANUARY 22, 1905, the *Augusta Chronicle* had good news to report for local baseball fans looking to the second season for the Tourists. The Philadelphia Athletics, the Detroit Tigers, and the University of Georgia's baseball team all would be playing practice games against the local favorites that spring at Warren Park. The story also noted another important piece of news: "Engle, McLaughlin, Whipple, Wilson and Cobb are the only ball players with Augusta last season who will be given a chance to make good on the local club this year. At an early date, the full retinue of players who have signed will be made public by Manager [Andy] Roth."

Fans also were told the grandstand and bleachers were being renovated for the new season with the addition of a no smoking section! The *Chronicle* noted, "The new arrangement whereby the side of the grandstand for the ladies is separated from that used by the smokers by the main entrance will be appreciated by the fairer sex who love the sport."

On January 29, 1905, the *Chronicle* ran a bold headline proclaiming, AUGUSTA'S STRING OF PLAYERS LOOK GOOD, with a subhead saying, EIGHTEEN MEN SIGNED AND MANAGER ROTH FISHING FOR SEVERAL OTHERS. The article reported that Tourists club president John B. Carter and manager Roth would pick fourteen players from the eighteen signed to contracts and listed the signed men as: Roth, catcher, utility or fielder; Lauzon, formerly of the Southern League; Dexter, first base; Engle or Nowell at second base; Meehan, Young, or Dunham at shortstop; Gilligan or Ruhlan, third base; outfielders, Smith, Wilson, Copeland, and Cobb; pitchers, McLaughlin, Whipple, Holmes, and Buchanan.

"From this bunch of promising men, Roth is confident that he will be able to select a team that will be heard from during the present season," the *Chronicle* said. "They are all good men with excellent records or are promising youngsters." President Carter also was quoted as saying, "If there is any weakness to be propped up, we will find it out early. It is our desire to give the local fans the best season of baseball they ever enjoyed."

In its brief profile of Cobb, the newspaper said, "Cobb is also one who is known to the fans, and Andy says that he will make 'Big Leaguer' timber out of him this year, as all the boy needs is competent handling."

On February 17, Augusta fans learned the Philadelphia Athletics led by manager Connie Mack would arrive on March 5, and begin practice the next day. They were expected to stay a week before leaving to begin a practice tour throughout the South.

The Detroit Tigers team, led by manager Bill Armour, was expected to arrive on March 7, and make Augusta the team's headquarters throughout its practice season. The team was to stay a month in the city before playing practice games in Augusta and elsewhere.

Manager Roth announced that he had scheduled practice games between the Tourists and the Detroit teams for April 3 and April 4 and, in addition, the Brooklyn Superbas (later known as the Dodgers) would be in Augusta on March 30 and April 1 to "cross bats" with the Detroit team.

The *Chronicle*, barely able to contain itself, noted that in just the one-week period that both the Detroit and Philadelphia teams would be in town, "local fans will be able to see at Warren Park during that period the largest collection of first-class ball tossers ever in Augusta at one time."

The first regular exhibition ball game of the season at which admission would be charged was played at Warren Park on March 20 at 4:15 p.m. between the Detroit and Augusta teams. Manager Roth was concerned about his minor leaguers going up against a major-league team in fair condition, but he felt confident "the boys will be able to give a good account of themselves."

Detroit manager Bill Armour also expected a good game, but said he was pretty certain his team would be victorious. "Judging by the men Roth has already on hand, Augusta has a good ball club," Armour said, sounding like a politician, "and while they cannot be expected to win from the Tigers, I am confident that they can make us play ball."

As it turned out, Armour was right, and Detroit did beat Augusta 6–0, with Cobb playing right field and only managing to get a base hit.

The next day, the two teams met again with Detroit again beating Augusta, this time 8–2. Cobb was cited for his "star work" in getting two base hits and scoring one of the two runs. And on the third match-up of the two teams the following day, Detroit again beat Augusta with the final score this time being 7–3, with Cobb getting only one base hit.

On March 24, the *Chronicle* gave Cobb mixed reviews and offered him a friendly piece of advice in writing, "Cobb is showing up well. Only one word of caution to the clever sticker in running bases, to wit: You are not in the amateur game now, and reckless endeavors to steal a sack on an experienced pitcher, when he has the ball, is a failure nine times out of ten. Fast sprinting, clever sliding and neat swings around the basemen, well practiced, will pay you better in the long run, Cobb."

The next day, the *Chronicle* predicted Cobb was a diamond in the rough and offered Roth the suggestion he should try Cobb more as a first baseman. The newspaper wrote, "For a short time yesterday afternoon, Cobb tried first base and pleased the fans. He is good on ground balls, fields cleanly all thrown balls and, in the opinion of many, would make an ideal first sacker. It is a tip for Manager Roth."

By the end of March, Roth had whipped his team into what was described as excellent condition. Amazingly, on the afternoon of March 28, they managed to beat the Tigers, 8–7. Cobb, back playing right field, got two base hits and scored one of the runs. The local fans yelled themselves hoarse at the good work of their hometown team. "From Augusta's standpoint, it was a great game," the *Chronicle* reported. "Not that anyone believes the locals can regularly defeat the major league team, but it showed the boys are hefty with the stick and that to win the opposing team, even though of the heavier caliber, must play the game for all it is worth. The youngsters were in the game from start to finish."

On the following day, Detroit trounced Augusta 9–1, but the series of games undoubtedly gave Detroit manager Armour a careful evaluation of Cobb's playing skills.

When the *Chronicle* profiled the 1905 team's individual players on April 16, the roster included manager Andy Roth of Philadelphia; first baseman C. V. Jordan of Baltimore, Maryland; second baseman Clyde Engle of Dayton, Ohio; third baseman Gus Ruhland, who started his professional career with the New York State league; shortstop Rabbit Meehan of Philadelphia; fielders T. W. Smith of Dayton, Ohio, and Ty Cobb of Royston, Georgia. The pitchers were Eddie Cicotte of Detroit;[6] Eddie McLaughlin of Oil City, Pennsylvania; J. F. Holmes, who started his pro career in the Kitty League; and Billie Battle of Rocky Mount, North Carolina. Ed Lauzon of Mobile, Alabama, was the catcher.

"I have been a long time in baseball," manager Roth commented, "but I have never played with a more confident or willing set of men. They want to see the Augusta team succeed, and, if they fail in putting us among the leaders, it will be because of inability—not because of indifference. . . . I have no fault to find with the condition of the men. They are ready to play ball. There is not a man who has failed to work hard."

To draw attention to the home opener on April 23, and give the local players some recognition, they were picked up by carriages at 3:00 p.m. in front of the Albion Hotel on the south side of the 700 block of Broad Street, were driven east on Broad to McKinnie (now 13th Street), then driven back west on Broad to Center (now Fifth Street), and finally driven a few blocks to Warren Park to begin play at 4:30 p.m.

The Tourists did win their season opening game, 2–1, against the Charleston (South Carolina) Sea Gulls before 2,000 fans in "perfect weather," on a squeeze play in the ninth inning. Cobb's performance in left field was nothing to write home about: He came to bat four times without getting a base

---

6 Eddie Cicotte, a native of Detroit, would play for the Detroit Tigers, Boston Red Sox, and the Chicago White Sox. As a member of the 1919 White Sox, Cicotte was accused with seven other players of fixing the Series so that the favored White Sox lost to the Cincinnati Reds. Cicotte signed a confession and received immunity but later recanted and was acquitted of all charges at trial by jury. He and his alleged coconspirators were banned from baseball for life by Commissioner Kenesaw Mountain Landis.

hit or scoring a run. In spite of Andy Roth's best efforts as both a player and manager and in spite of his role in getting Cobb back on the Tourists roster, the team went into a slump by midseason, and in July, Andy Roth stepped down as manager and player George Leidy was promoted. Roth would remain with the team, but Leidy now would be calling the shots. "In taking charge, Manager Leidy made no rash promises," the newspaper said, "simply declaring that he would use his best endeavors and baseball knowledge to get the team back on a winning streak."

Front office and managerial changes didn't help pull the Tourists out of their slump, and Leidy was removed as manager by new club president C. D. Carr less than a month later, on August 15. Andy Roth was again promoted to manager.

Carr told reporters, "Leidy has unquestionably done his best as the manager and failed. I wish to say for him that he has treated us cleverly and squarely. I will also say that I believe that he has done his best to get together a winning team. He failed, and we felt that a change was necessary."

However rough things were for the team, the month of August had started incredibly well for Cobb. The Royston teenager had become the first player in the SALLY League to attain one hundred base hits. Then things took a devastating turn. On the morning of Wednesday, August 9, 1905, while staying at the Albion Hotel on Broad Street in Augusta, Cobb received the news that his mother had shot and killed his father outside their home in Royston the previous night.

No one ever knew for certain what happened on that tragic night, but the investigating coroner's jury in Franklin County was told that Ty's father, W. H. Cobb, had told his wife, Amanda, that he was going out of town on a business trip, but that he had instead driven his horse and buggy to a farm he owned outside of town where he left them while he walked back to downtown Royston where Mrs. Cobb was home alone.[7] He was seen in Royston at about 10:00 p.m., but it was said by a witness that he seemed to be trying to hide his identity.

---

7 The two younger Cobb children, Paul (just a year younger than his brother, Ty), and Florence, were staying overnight with friends.

Mrs. Cobb gave her version of the shooting at the coroner's inquest: "I retired about ten-thirty o'clock and woke up some time during the night. I heard a kind of rustling noise at the lower window of my room. I got up and got my pistol. I saw a form some distance from the window. As it went behind the chimney, I went to the upper window.

"I went from window to window two or three times, maybe more. The form seemed to get nearer to the upper window and I pulled down the shade so that I could see just below it. The form seemed to crouch down. I stood at the upper side of the window and pulled the shade to one side and shot twice.

"After shooting, I thought everything. I began to scream and went to send Clifford Ginn[8] after a doctor. I called Mr. Wellborn. I couldn't call very loud. After shooting, I threw the pistol down. I don't know how long it was between [shots]."

The *Augusta Chronicle* wrote a long, innuendo-filled article about the shooting: "Professor Cobb had received notice about two weeks since that he had better watch his home," the *Chronicle* stated. "Before the date of the tragedy which cost the life of the husband, it is alleged there had been more than one disagreement between himself and his wife, and owing to the various rumors and reports, sensational developments are expected.

"Mrs. Cobb's statement that she mistook her husband for a burglar is doubted by many," the article continued. "It is the general opinion that when Professor Cobb went away, ostensibly to be gone several days, he returned unexpectedly and that the killing followed. It is believed, however, that Mrs. Cobb did the shooting."

The newspaper further noted, "No male person other than Professor Cobb was seen at the Cobb home that night, so far as known," but the article did add that "witnesses were introduced who testified there was a considerable interval between the shots, sufficient time for a person to walk back and forth across a room."

---

8 Ginn was about four years older than Ty Cobb, and he had played on the Royston Reds baseball team with Cobb. Ginn was married to Amanda's sister, Eunice, who was only a year older than Cobb.

Dr. J. O. McCrary, the physician who was called to the shooting site, testified to the coroner's jury that he found a revolver and a rock in the victim's pockets, either Cobb expected to confront someone back at his home, or else he may just have taken the revolver along as usual as protection on his late evening buggy trips. It was not uncommon for travelers to carry pistols or rocks for protection at night. Some experts believe that it was not possible that Amanda Cobb might have had a lover, due to the closeness of other houses. In any case, Professor Cobb would not have expected to encounter his wife's lover in his house that night even if she did have one.

Still, some people questioned Amanda Cobb's relationship with Clifford Ginn, the first person she called after the shooting. Following the shooting, Clifford Ginn's relationship with the Cobb family would become even more important. He became the legal guardian of Ty Cobb (who was still a minor) and his two siblings, and the Ginn home became home to the Cobb children, and especially Ty, on his trips home to Royston.

As for the other man Amanda called for help after the shooting and only identified as "Wellborn" in her testimony, expert Fricks said he was Curtis B. Wellborn Sr., who lived a short ways down the street from the Cobb family home and "was an elder gentleman that people in the neighborhood looked up to."

Understandably, the three Cobb children were upset with the way their mother was being portrayed in newspapers as a possibly cheating wife who might have recognized their father before she shot him, therefore knowing that he wasn't really a burglar.

The *Chronicle* headlined a brief story on August 13, saying, COBB CHILDREN DENY REPORTS, with that account noting, "Paul and Florence Cobb, children of Mr. and Mrs. Cobb, say in an interview that they were much surprised to see the sensational reports in regard to family differences between their father and mother. Paul said that the domestic relations between his father and mother were the most pleasant in that they lived together in perfect harmony and the reports are absolutely untrue."

Nevertheless, Mrs. Cobb was charged with voluntary manslaughter after the coroner's jury inquest and released on a $7,000 bond. Her trial was expected to take place the next month.

Meanwhile back in Augusta, fans and friends of Cobb were sympathetic about what he was going through and were eager to have him return to the Tourists. The *Chronicle* noted, "Efforts are being made to get Cobb back to his post, one of the players remarking last night that the team without Cobb is like an army without a Washington or Lee."

But, as it would turn out, the days were numbered for Cobb's being a member of the Augusta Tourists team. On August 14, the *Chronicle* published a story headlined, Sizing-Up Cobb. It said a major-league scout, apparently unaware that Cobb was in Royston with his family, was spotted in Jacksonville, Florida, hoping to see Cobb play.

"It is known that a certain American league team needing strengthening last week sent a man all the way to Jacksonville just to see Cobb at work. The killing of his father prevented the youngster from being watched without knowing it. Understanding that Cobb would report in time for the Friday or Saturday game at Savannah, the hunter for promising players followed the team only to be again disappointed. It is understood that he is scouting about in this section watching to see when the youngster is again at work.

"Cobb's record, second in batting in the league, a run-getter and fast on his feet combined with the fact that he is a comer yet in his teens, is one that shows that he has fast company timber to develop. Augusta is sure to lose his services next season."

With Cobb's mother out on bail awaiting trial, he left Royston by train on the afternoon of August 15, and arrived in Augusta the next morning in time to play in a doubleheader with the Charleston Sea Gulls. The news accounts the next day reported Cobb played left field in both games and had two base hits in the first but didn't score any runs. The Tourists lost that game, 3–0. Cobb started in the second game but had to leave due to an injured finger. Even though he went without a hit, the Tourists still won the second game, 2–1.

Four days after Cobb's return to the Tourists, Augusta baseball fans woke on August 20 to see the headline:

Tyrus Cobb Sold to Detroit Club.

Fans were told in the article, "It is understood that they surely dreaded for the future success of their team even if it did mean taking pride in what was happening to one of the team's star players. The price paid by [Detroit Tigers] Manager Armour was $500. The purchase was unconditional in that the money comes to the Augusta management in a lump, and the purchaser takes all chances of the youngster proving fit material for faster company. However, there is no question among the fans of the South Atlantic League that Cobb will make good and that Armour has picked up a 'find.'"

Cobb's last day with the Tourists actually was August 25. The Augusta fans did their best to show how much they appreciated his efforts in presenting him with "a handsome gold watch" and a bunch of roses.

"The watch and fob were presents from the fans of the city and the baseball club," the *Chronicle* reported. "The flowers were the gift of a young lady. Time was called during the game for the presentations. Mr. John R. Burke presented the watch and fob in a short speech, wishing the young player well in faster company."

However, Cobb did not leave the city for Detroit immediately after the game as expected. Cobb wanted a share of his purchase price of $500 and was reportedly unhappy with the salary offered in Detroit. His concerns were apparently addressed, and Cobb wore a Detroit uniform for the first time as a Tigers player less than a week later on August 30.

As 1905 came to a close, Cobb was firmly berthed on a major-league team and was on the fast track toward becoming an international sports legend, but the threat of his mother's being convicted of his father's murder hung over the eighteen-year-old sports prodigy's head.

# Tyrus Raymond Cobb: The Early Years 3

If you are ever up in northern Georgia just south of the small town of Cornelia and get on Georgia Highway 105—also designated as Ty Cobb Parkway—heading for Carnesville, you will soon within a few miles pass by an area known as "The Narrows" that doesn't appear on most Georgia road maps. If you're sharp, you'll see on the right a large metal sign that proclaims, Birthplace of Ty Cobb. The Georgia Peach. December 18, 1886.

According to former Cornelia resident Pope Welborn, who knew Cobb in his final years, Cobb took him to The Narrows and pointed out the exact area where he was born. "He told me his mother was a Chitwood, and she and Herschel [Cobb's father] came by buggy for the birth on his grandparents' property [Amanda's parents]. He said that everybody always said Ty Cobb was born in the Chitwood house that stood on the south side of the road, but he said, 'I wasn't, and I remember my parents telling me that I was born in a log cabin that stood a long time in a pasture across the road.'"

The Narrows community is in Banks County, which was created by the Georgia General Assembly on December 11, 1858, from land in Franklin, Habersham, Jackson, and Hall Counties, and named for Richard E. Banks, a doctor known for his kindness to the Cherokees in Georgia and South Carolina. The Narrows is noted for a Civil War battle, the details of which are on a Georgia Historical Society marker in a city park in nearby Baldwin.

Cobb's first name of Tyrus came from the city of Tyre, Phoenicia (now Lebanon), where Tyre's fierce-fighting citizens held off an attack by Alexander the Great, who wanted the city for a strategic coastal base during a war between the Greeks and the Persians, for seven months in 332 B.C. Alexander destroyed half of Tyre and either killed or sold into slavery its 30,000 residents. As an adult, Ty Cobb was fascinated with Alexander the Great and was known to have read many books about the military leader as well as those about another famous conqueror, Napoleon of France.

Cobb himself was distantly related to another military hero, Howell Cobb (1815–1868), who was a major general in the Confederate rebel army and who also served as a U.S. congressman, Speaker of the U.S. House of Representatives, governor of Georgia, secretary of the U.S. treasury, and president of the Confederate Provisional Congress.

He also was related to another Confederate general, Howell's younger brother, Thomas Reade Rootes Cobb (1823–1862), who also was a lawyer who edited twenty volumes of Georgia Supreme Court reports, prepared *A Digest of the Statute Laws of the State of Georgia*, and compiled a new state criminal code. In the early months of the Civil War, in August of 1861, Cobb gave up his law practice and formed a regiment of infantry, cavalry, and artillery known as "Cobb's Legion." Cobb was killed in December 1862, barely a year into the war, at the battle of Fredericksburg, Virginia. There is a statue of him on the Confederate monument in downtown Augusta that his distant relative, Ty Cobb, would walk and drive by many times.

Ty's parents, William Herschel Cobb and Amanda Chitwood Cobb, married on February 11, 1886, ten months before his birth, according to the marriage license filed in the Banks County courthouse in the county seat of Homer. His father, born on February 23, 1863, during the Civil War, was at the time of his marriage a schoolteacher and twelve days shy of his twenty-third birthday. His mother was born January 15, 1871, and was fifteen years old at the time of her wedding.

Ty's only brother, John Paul, who also would become a professional baseball player, was born a little over two years after Ty on February 23, 1889, and his only sister, Florence Leslie, was born on October 29, 1892.

To better provide for his growing family, Cobb's schoolteacher father moved the family to Carnesville, the county seat of Franklin County, between Cornelia and Royston, before moving them to Royston when Ty was about five or six. Cobb's father climbed social, business, and political ladders. He taught math and was the principal of schools in Lavonia, Harmony Grove, Carnesville, and Royston. He became the editor of the *Royston Record* newspaper and, as a state senator, introduced legislation in the Georgia Senate to set up a system of country schools throughout the state. He also became a school commissioner of Franklin County.

As with many rural youths, Cobb enjoyed hunting and fishing. He accidentally shot himself with a .22-caliber rifle when he was about fourteen or fifteen. Cobb said he was helping butcher hogs when he set his rifle against a tree. He reached to grab it, and a branch caught the trigger causing the gun to fire a bullet into Cobb's collarbone. His father rushed him to Atlanta, but doctors could not find the bullet. Cobb contended it remained somewhere in his body the rest of his life.

Cobb said his father let him write at least one editorial for the *Royston Record*, and he also claimed to have "borrowed" two of his father's expensive library books to trade for a baseball glove at a local store. He loved woodworking and made his own bats with machinery owned by the father of his friend, Joe Cunningham. The black bat that he used during his Augusta Tourist practices in 1904 might have been made by Ty himself.

Cobb's father wrote him a beautifully worded letter on stationery of the Board of Education of Franklin County on January 5, 1902, a little more than two years before Ty left Royston to play ball in Augusta, while Ty was in North Carolina visiting relatives over the Christmas holidays. It read:

*Tyrus, Dear Boy —*
*The first snow of the year of account is down today. It is two inches I reckon. It is all of a round fine hail not a single feathery flake, some lodge on the limbs of the trees. Our wheat and oats have stood the winter all right, wheat is up nicely. We are all snowed in today principally because of the cold weather. Hardly a sound has been heard today. It is nearly six o'clock. I knew the past cold weather would furnish you with*

*some fine scenery up there and I am glad you have been receptive of its austere beauty and solemn grandeur, as to color, sound, and picturesque contour or outline. That is a picturesque and romantic country with solitude enough to give nature a chance to be heard in the soul. The presence of man and the jargon of artificiality and show do not crowd out the grand aspect of God's handiwork among those everlasting hills covered with its primeval forest, [do] not hush the grand oratorios of the winds, nor check the rush of her living leaping waters.*

*To be educated is not only to be master of the printed page but be able to catch the messages of star, rock, flower, bird, painting and symphony. To have eyes that really see, ears that really hear and an imagination that can construct the perfect from a fragment. It is truly great to have a mind that will respond to and open the door of the soul to all the legions of thoughts and symbols of knowledge and emotions that the whole universe around us brings to us.*

*Be good and dutiful, conquer your anger and passions that would degrade your dignity and belittle your manhood. Cherish all the good that springs up in you. Be under the perpetual guidance of the better angel of your nature. Starve out and drive out the demon that lurks in all human blood and ready and anxious and restless to arise and reign.*

*Be good.*
*Yours affectionately,*
*W. H. COBB*

There has been speculation as to whether or not Cobb's father supported his son's baseball playing ambitions. It is probably true Cobb's father and mother would have preferred he become a doctor or lawyer or educator, but there was no family rift after he became a ball player. The *Augusta Chronicle* reported on April 18, 1904, "Cobb is expecting his father in a few days." More printed evidence of the affection Cobb's parents had for him is an article published in the *Chronicle* on February 16, 1919, headlined, Ty Cobb's Childhood/ Recalled By Mother/ To Atlanta Reporter. It read in part as follows:

"When Ty Cobb was five years old he earned twenty-five cents by driving a neighbor's cow to pasture for him. And how do you guess he invested his earnings? He bought a baseball mitt! . . .

"Mrs. Cobb, of course, has seen her son play big league ball many, many times, and she is a great lover of the game.

"'I had rather see Ty play than anybody,' she said, 'and I don't think it is all maternal pride either. I try to forget I am his mother and even when I watch him with unprejudiced eyes I am constrained to believe he is a pretty good ball player.

"'Ty always has been impetuous and headstrong. Even when he was just a little tot in short clothes he hated to lose an argument, and he never did lose many. He was full of mischief in his boyhood days, and he had fights in school. If a stronger boy would get the best of him, Ty would fight him every day or two until he won the verdict. He would never give up or admit a lad could get the best of him.

"'His father and I were very much opposed to playing professional ball at first, but his mind was so set on it that I relented. I felt that a man should go into whatever walk of life his heart was set upon.

"'The thing that always impressed me most about Ty's playing is the speed he gets away to the bases. When he hits the ball, I have noticed that he is always about three or four steps towards first base before his bat hits the ground. He makes a lot of bases by beating out infield hits.

"'I don't think there is any doubt about Ty playing for Detroit again this year,' said Mrs. Cobb. 'He has talked about quitting baseball, but it will be mighty hard for him to do so.'"

# Amanda Cobb Goes on Trial 4

The year 1906 would be a transitional—and emotional—one for Ty Cobb as he began his first full year in the major leagues playing with the Detroit Tigers, while mentally preparing for his mother's trial, charged with the murder of his father.

Cobb was back in Augusta on January 17, 1906, spending some days with his friends and admirers. The *Augusta Chronicle* noted that Cobb had good things to say about how he was being treated by the Detroit Tigers management, including receiving a "much better contract" that was already "signed, sealed, and delivered" for the coming season.

"Cobb is larger and broader-shouldered than last season," the newspaper observed, "and by the time he reaches his majority will no doubt be a husky man. He is in very fine condition and is confident of making good this year, being anxious for the time when [Detroit manager Bill] Armour's tribe shall gather in Augusta for their preliminary practice."

He stayed in Augusta at least until early February and apparently was on a special assignment for Armour, checking to see if the Warren Park ball field was in good shape for the Tigers spring practice. Cobb found some problems with the field that needed correcting, noting that "the outfield is boggy, full of holes and thoroughly covered with trash."

Cobb's concerns about the park were taken to heart and the problems corrected. The Tigers were back in Augusta playing and beating the Brooklyn Superbas of the National League, 12–5, on March 21, with Cobb playing center field and hitting two home runs. The elation Cobb felt over his excellent showings in spring training with the Tigers must have been countered by his personal feelings about his mother's impending trial that same month.

The trial was held in Lavonia, Georgia, beginning at 3:00 p.m. on Friday, March 30, and mercifully lasted only two days. Amanda Chitwood Cobb had some powerful legal representation on her side. Her attorneys were the high-profile leaders from several Georgia cities: J. C. Thomas of Athens, Judge W. R. Little of Carnesville, Col. H. H. Chandler of Lavonia, Col. Worley Adams of Royston, and Col. R. A. E. Hamby of Clayton.

Prosecuting the case for the state of Georgia were its solicitor general, S. J. Tribble of Athens, Hon. A. J. Curry, Hon. Julian Curry of Hartwell, and Col. T. G. Dorough of Royston.

"There is an enormous crowd of people in attendance upon the trial and a fight for every inch of ground will be made," the *Chronicle* reported. "The case is the most important one that has been tried in this court for a number of years owing to the prominence of Professor W. H. Cobb and his wife in the community."

Following the second and final day of the trial, the *Chronicle* published a story saying the highlight of the previous day had been Mrs. Cobb herself taking the witness stand. Her voice was described as plainly heard throughout the courtroom as she made a "very long" statement about what happened. The story added, "She emphatically denied knowing at whom she shot at the time, and claimed that she mistook her husband for a burglar."

On April 1, 1906, the *Chronicle* headline was no joke: MRS. COBB FREE; JURY ACQUITS. The all-male jury had deliberated an hour and forty minutes before finding her innocent. Mrs. Cobb returned to her home in nearby Royston "immediately after the verdict was rendered," readers were told.

Since that incident, there has been much written and speculated as to how this family tragedy affected the later life of Ty Cobb. Cobb apparently didn't blame his mother for his father's death or didn't have harsh feelings toward her, because we know from accounts in the *Chronicle* and elsewhere she came to visit his family in Augusta, she saw him play whenever she could, and that he took care of his mother and his single sister throughout the rest of their lives. Amanda Chitwood Cobb died at age sixty-six at her home in Atlanta on October 19, 1936. (Years later Cobb built a large mausoleum in the Rose Hill cemetery in Royston and had his mother and father and sister reinterred there.)

In the same issue of April 1, 1906, that the *Chronicle* announced the verdict of Amanda Cobb's trial, it also had a brief item in which the newspaper for the first time used the term "Georgia Peach" in reference to Cobb. The *Chronicle* offered a "Cobblet" from a local resident named Joe Jackson who said, "Ty Cobb, the Georgia Peach or the Georgia Cracker, is the only one who has the whole town with him. If Tyrus had fewer friends it would save the newspaper men many steps."

As he went into that 1906 season, Cobb reportedly received a great deal of "new guy" hazing from his fellow Detroit teammates, especially from Matty McIntyre of Stonington, Connecticut, who was six years older than Cobb. McIntyre led a couple of other teammates in throwing wet wads of newspapers at Cobb from behind, smashing the crowns out of his hats, sawing his homemade bats in half, and egging him into fistfights. As a result by mid-July, Cobb had developed such a major case of stomach ulcers that he would be out of playing for nearly two months, finally returning to the Tigers in early September.

The *Chronicle* put Cobb's physical situation into a clearer picture by noting in an article of August 1, 1906, how the game of baseball took its toll on other professional players as well. "According to some of the northern papers there have been a number of the big league players out of the game this year on account of injuries or sickness," the article observed.

"It is said that Ty Cobb is out of the game on account of stomach trouble. Some of his friends here say that he is getting different eating from what he has been used to, and if [Detroit Tigers] Manager Armour will feed him blue-stem collards and corn bread that Cobb will make him a good man.

"Cobb is a fine boy, and there are hundreds of fans here who would be glad to see him in one of the outer gardens. Cobb is too valuable a man, however, for anything like this to be done, as he is being saved now for reserve work, although he is on the sick list."

Even though Cobb would play for only another month before the season ended, the *Chronicle* reported on November 2, 1906, when he was back visiting friends in Augusta, that Cobb still had ended the season with the fourth-best batting average in the American League. The National Baseball Hall of Fame lists Cobb's 1906 batting average of .316, playing ninety-eight games, with 350 at bats. In those games he racked up 45 runs, 112 hits, 1 home run, and 23 stolen bases.

The *Augusta Herald* noted of Cobb's return visit in November of 1906 that he was taking in the sights of the Georgia-Carolina Fair and was busy "shaking hands with a host of friends." The *Herald* added, "Cobb is very glad to get back among his friends in Augusta and says that, although he has played in many cities, still Augusta is always the one nearest his heart."

Just a few days later, on November 18, the *Chronicle* told its readers more about Augusta's hold on Cobb's heart saying, "Tyrus Cobb was here recently for the purpose of opening up a first-class gentleman's pool room but was unable to secure the proper location. He will return within the next month or so and renew negotiations. At any rate, he will spend several months of the winter here, and intends to be here when the Detroit team comes for its spring training."

And on December 4, the *Chronicle* not only again spoke of Cobb's seemingly permanent spot on the Detroit Tigers team but also mentioned his teammate, Matty McIntyre, who had made Cobb's life such a living hell even as he was going through the heartache of his father's death and mother's trial. "While in Augusta several weeks ago, Cobb spoke confidently of being with the Detroit team next year," the *Chronicle* reported, "and said that he had received strong assurances to this effect from [new Detroit manager] Hughie Jennings. It is probable, however, that some arrangement will be made whereby he and McIntyre will be separated, as last year there was considerable fiction between them, neither willing to assist the other in any way whatever."

# THE FIGHTING SIDE OF COBB       5

IN 1907, WITH HIS MOTHER'S ORDEAL SETTLED and his first full year with the Detroit Tigers behind him, Ty Cobb set about the business of being Ty Cobb as the Tigers, led by manager Hughie Jennings, returned to Augusta in mid-March for spring training. Returning for a third spring training at Warren Park, the Tigers again encountered warm feelings from both the local people and local press.

"The weather has been ideal for practice and Jennings has taken every advantage that the Augusta climate has offered," the *Augusta Chronicle* reported on March 16. "His entire team is beginning to look like it does in July when New York or some other team is played on a Northern diamond. Manager Jennings and his players have made many friends during their stay in Augusta and during the remainder of their stay here will continue to be popular. They all declare that the Augusta climate cannot be equaled anywhere."

Just four days after arriving in Augusta for spring training of 1907, Cobb's quick temper raised its ugly head in the first of what would be many incidents of violent behavior reported by the press, even in his friendly "hometown" newspapers, throughout the ball player's career. The afternoon *Augusta Herald* reprinted an article by Paul H. Bruske of the *Detroit Times* in which Bruske wrote, "The trouble today started in an altercation between

Cobb and several negroes. One negro who knew Cobb when the player was with the Augusta club attempted to shake hands with him as he reached the field for the afternoon practice, but when the negro addressed him with the remark, 'Herro, Carrie,' Cobb started in immediate pursuit. The negro rushed into the house of the negro groundskeeper nearby and Cobb followed. In the fracas which ensued, the wife of the groundskeeper took a lively hand, making so much vocal ado that, when Cobb emerged, his team mates were gathered round the door.

"[Catcher Charlie] Schmidt criticized Cobb for his supposed assault on the woman and the latter, who is a Georgian, without explaining the situation, told Schmidt to mind his own business. They mixed immediately, Schmidt landing a hard right to the face and blocking Cobb's lead. They clinched and wrestled for some time exchanging short arm blows, and Cobb made a bloody network of Schmidt's face with his fingernails. Neither did further damage as Manager Jennings and the players separated them."

As result of the incident Jennings announced Cobb's release from the Tigers, saying he "is on the market and will be disposed to the highest bidder," regardless of the fact that Cobb had batted .316 in the American League in the 1906 season. Cobb was reportedly happy about reports that he was to be traded to the Cleveland club for Elmer Flick.

As it turned out, manager Jennings had received a telegram from Cleveland's manager, Larry Lajoie, who said he wanted Cobb for the team but didn't want to give up Flick for him. So, it was resolved Cobb would remain with the Tigers until a suitable deal could be made to transfer him to another club. "The difficulty between the Georgian and Catcher Schmidt has been smoothed over and these men will not have any more trouble," the *Chronicle* reported on March 18.

That spring the Tigers also went to Meridian, Mississippi, to train and that first afternoon of training, Schmidt and Cobb got into it again, with Schmidt giving Cobb a black eye. The *Augusta Herald* ran a story by M.W. Bingay of the *Detroit News* saying that Hughie Jennings took the two fighting players into the parlor of the hotel where they were staying, talked to them in a calm voice, and, rather than chewing them out, handed them some salve for their bruises. Jennings said he was an old man in the game and didn't care about harmony on the team but that they should. "'You can win that pennant," Jennings was quoted as saying, "and to do it we have got to have harmony. You've got to work with me. I want every man here to agree that we will work together and stamp out all this nonsense. Let's act like men and not like schoolboys."

Bingay also wrote that incident in Meridian was the start of the Tigers coming together into being a fighting machine that would startle the world of baseball.

Cobb was becoming known as a fighting machine on his own. As the 1907 season came to a close, the *Chronicle* reported that while the Tigers were playing against Cleveland recently, two detectives were with Cobb to keep Harry Bemis, Cleveland's shortstop, "from doing the Georgia boy harm."

The account further noted, "Bemis was spiked during a game in Cleveland by Cobb and was out of the game a good while. Bemis says Cobb spiked him on purpose. Cobb says he didn't. That's the way the thing started, and now the entire Cleveland team, excepting probably a few of the older and cooler heads, are after Cobb's scalp. You can count on Cobb doing his part, however, for he can whip nearly any man in the two big leagues."

As 1907 came to a close, instead of being in a fight, Cobb actually was the referee of a fight of sorts, the event being a championship wrestling match in Augusta between Pete Douglas and Al Christenson on November 7, 1907, in the Grand Opera House at the corner of Jackson (Eighth) and Greene Streets. An estimated 300 turned out to see the event, which started late due to Christenson's manager being late. But the orchestra of Augusta Tourist rooter Señor Jose Andonegui was there and kept the audience entertained until the manager arrived.

"About 9 o'clock, Ty Cobb, to great applause and wearing a neat white sweater, announced the approaching bout as a catch-as-catch-can, best two-out-of-three falls, strangle-hold barred," the *Chronicle* reported. "Then the doughty warriors came on."

Christenson ended up taking the match by winning two of the three falls.

The next month, Cobb ended up joining the YMCA baseball team in

Augusta to play an indoor game in the Armory against a team from the Knights of Columbus. Cobb played right field, and, at his first time at bat in the first inning hit a grounder, but, as the *Herald* reported, "the slick floor of the armory bewildered him and he died on first." Typically, Cobb got the hang of things pretty quick and, before the game ended 6–5 in favor of the YMCA team, got 2 hits and scored one run.

While Cobb was a hit with most of the spectators judging by the cheering, one local baseball fan, John J. Heffernan, wrote the *Herald* that the game should be thrown out in the interest of fair play because the YMCA team had a one-sided advantage by using a professional ballplayer who was "the whole show."

On the same page as Heffernan's letter, a *Herald* sports columnist identified as "H. F. A." responded by writing, "The playing of Ty Cobb with the Y.M.C.A. team means nothing. He had just as soon play with the weakest team in the league. What he wants is to keep in shape for his games next summer. All the big players in the country try to get all the practice they can in the winter months and Cobb concluded the indoor baseball league was just the thing for him."

More and more, whether it was playing indoor baseball with a bunch of YMCA amateurs or outdoor baseball with major-league players, Cobb definitely was emerging from the dark days of his father's death and mother's trial and was enjoying life to the fullest.

And, so what do you do when you're single and you are making national headlines after only two years playing with a major-league team?

Why get married, of course.

# FIFTEEN HOURS IN AUGUSTA      6

DETROIT FANS ATTENDING THEIR HOME GAME on August 9, 1908, in Bennett Park were far more interested in what was going on in the stands than what was going on in the field—all because of a simple little ceremony that had taken place three days earlier in a Victorian-style house outside of Augusta, Georgia: the wedding of the man who would become the world's greatest baseball player to the eldest daughter of one of Augusta's most prominent families.

The August 10 article in the *Augusta Herald* with the dateline of Detroit and headlined, MRS. COBB COULD NOT LEAVE FIELD, offered this account of what happened in the game against the Washington Senators:

"Mrs. Tyrus Raymond Cobb, formerly Miss Charlie Lombard of Augusta, Ga., had a little more strenuous reception upon her first appearance here than was planned.

"The bride of the champion batter sat in the stand yesterday afternoon with his mother, watching her husband on the diamond for the first time [at least the first time in Detroit]. She was not discovered until the fifth inning when Tyrus smashed out a three bagger to left that brought forth all his spectacular speed.

"He looked toward her, and the thousands took the cue. The trim little girl, heavily veiled, was given an ovation. Thousands stood in the stands and watched her. When it was all over, she found she could not leave the park, for at every exit a mighty throng awaited her.

"The ground keeper managed to lock the gates, but the mob refused to disperse. A carriage was called and the Georgian with his bride, mother and little sister, after a half hour of waiting, managed to escape through a little doorway in the right field fence."

Ty Cobb had started 1908 by asking for and getting a salary boost to $5,000 for the new season. His salary for the 1907 season reportedly had been $1,500 a year, which was considered pretty good for a rookie player. But in January, Cobb was a contract holdout, stating: "It's a purely business proposition with me, for if I don't make all I can now, I will never have the chance again."

Cobb continued: "You see the best part of my life is being spent in playing the game, and it is impossible to study and learn any other profession without giving up professional baseball entirely. In summer, I find that I cannot read without injury to my eyes and corresponding injury to my batting average. Last spring I started on the road with novels and other literature but had to give them up. I even cannot read much in the newspapers without feeling its effect on my sight, so you see it doesn't pay to take chances.

"As I was saying, we can't study in the summer and we have but little time in the winter. It is November before we are off on the road, and then a few weeks to visit friends sees it well along into the winter, too late to think of entering college. Back to work in March and then hard work until fall again. So you can readily see that I am justified in asking for $5,000. The best years of my life are being devoted to the game, and if I don't make my maximum salary right now, I never will get above the sum offered me."

The twenty-year-old Cobb was justified in asking for an increase in pay because of his excellent record during the 1907 season. He had played in 150 games, batting 605 times. He scored 97 runs on 212 hits, hit 5 home runs, stole 49 bases, and ended the season with a batting average of .350.

One of his biggest supporters was "Wild Bill" Donovan, the Detroit Tiger who had led the American League pitchers in the 1907 season. He was quoted in an article published February 1, 1908, in the *Herald* as saying, "I'll tell you something that you can gamble on. This Ty Cobb is a little bit the best ball player in the world. There isn't any thing to that proposition. I've been playing big league ball now for a good many years, and I have never seen the man in his class. When it comes to playing the game all the time he is there 40 ways. And the best of it is, he is just beginning. He will be better than ever next season and will continue to improve right along for several years."

Cobb's batting expertise and growing fame were such that in 1908 he became only the second player whose autograph was engraved onto a Louisville Slugger bat. In 1905 the Kentucky company had added Honus Wagner's signature to its bats. [9] The Detroit management agreed to Cobb's salary increase request, and a brief article in the *Augusta Herald* reporting on the momentous news said Cobb gave credit to M.W. Bingay, sports editor of the *Detroit News*, and Tom Hamilton, sports editor of the *Herald*, for assisting in negotiating his new salary with Detroit manager Hughie Jennings.

Hamilton, in fact, had sent a telegraph to sports editor Bingay in Hot Springs, Arkansas, who was there covering the Tigers already in spring training, saying, "Believe Cobb will accept straight one-year contract for five thousand dollars, but not a cent less. Inform Jennings and wire. This is confidential."

Cobb, it turned out, had an even more legitimate and pressing reason for wanting to increase his salary and his prospects in 1908—his very secret impending marriage to Charlie Marion Lombard. [10]

The well-liked Augusta woman very well may have been known to most Augustans and certainly had a higher social standing than her new husband when they married in the summer of 1908. Her family was filled with achievers who permeated almost every aspect of Augusta's business, religious, and recreational life.

Charlie, the youngest of the four Lombard children, was born on July 3,

---

9 Wagner was among the first five players inducted into the National Baseball Hall of Fame along with Cobb. According to the Louisville Slugger company, Wagner's signature was the first to be used on any manufactured bat, and that signature made Wagner the first professional athlete known to endorse a retail product.

10 It's easy to tell when some biographers or museum curators have not done their homework on the Lombard family, because they will list Ty's wife as "Charlotte" rather than using her real name, "Charlie."

1890, and was named for her father's uncle, Charles F. Lombard. He was a local civic leader and the owner of Burch's swimming pond, a popular destination four miles from Augusta.[11]

Charlie's grandfather, George Obed Lombard, had married Frances Rowley, daughter of Harmon Rowley, who had started a huge Richmond County company, incorporated in 1894 as Lombard Iron Works. George and Frances Lombard had two sons: George Rowley Lombard, born in Richmond County on New Year's Day of 1856, and Roswell Oliver Lombard, born in Richmond County on New Year's Day of 1860.

George R. Lombard developed Lombard Iron Works into a first-class, widely respected industrial company, while his brother, Roswell, became a community leader, the builder of one of Augusta's greatest theaters and, of course, Ty Cobb's father-in-law. Roswell also ran a successful gristmill nine miles from Augusta just off Dean's Bridge Road at Butler Creek.

Very little was mentioned of Cobb's love life in the local or national media prior to the news that he was getting married. We don't know for sure, but it's a pretty good bet Charlie was the "young lady" who presented Ty with roses on his last night as an Augusta Tourists player on August 25, 1905. Tom Hamilton (who had become the *Chronicle*'s sports editor in late 1908) told his readers that "the two have been sweethearts ever since Ty was a greenhorn ball player."

According to Ty and Charlie's daughter, Beverly, Charlie had gone to a Catholic girl's convent in Augusta (most likely Sacred Heart Academy at 1264 Ellis Street) and that the brother of a friend of Charlie's at the convent had introduced them. By late July 1908, the word was out they intended to marry the very next month.

Like most of the major events in Cobb's life, the news was printed on the front page of the *Augusta Chronicle*. On July 23, the headline read, TY COBB TO BE MARRIED TO AN AUGUSTA LADY. The *Chronicle* also reprinted an article from the *Washington Post* that said, "It has leaked out that Tyrus and Miss Charlie Lombard, an estimable young lady of Augusta, Ga., are to be joined in wedlock the first week in August. The wedding will take place

---

11 Eventually, recreational swimmers in the Augusta area came to know Burch Place Bathing Pond as Lombard's Pond.

in Augusta. Cobb already has obtained a leave of absence from Manager Jennings for a week for the purpose of entering into the life contract."

The *Montgomery (AL) Advertiser* offered, "One Tyrus Cobb, the distinguished Georgian champion batter and base runner of the American League, has gone and done it; or to be more exact he's going to make the greatest play of his life some time during the first week in August. His latest stunt will not take place on the diamond, instead, the stunt is scheduled for a decision at the altar. Cobb is going to get married, and his bride-to-be is Miss Charlie Lombard of Augusta, Ga. If Ty is as successful in the matrimonial game as he has been in baseball he can count himself in the '.400.'"

Sports editor Hamilton told Augusta readers, "He is a Southern gentleman and is about to be mated to a Southern lady. Now when the readers of this recall what it means to be a Southern gentleman and a Southern lady, they can understand. The personal congratulations to Ty and his bride are extended by the writer and all of us hope that theirs indeed be a pleasant journey through life."

The wedding would take place at high noon on August 6, at "The Oaks," the Lombard's large Victorian mansion at Butler Creek, nine miles from downtown Augusta, near the intersection of Old U.S. Highway 1 and Deans Bridge Road. The wedding itself was small and quiet, but it was covered on both the society page and the sports page. Articles before the wedding gushed about its importance and noted, "There has probably never been a marriage in Augusta that has been of more widespread interest than that of Miss Charlie Lombard and Ty Cobb. . . . Mr. Cobb's prominence in the sporting world coupled with his very pronounced popularity, together with his marriage—national affair, as it were, and everybody who knows anything of what he has done in the baseball world feels a personal interest in the romance the culmination of which will almost make him an Augustan."

*Chronicle* editor Tom Hamilton, apparently the only media person present at the ceremony, wrote this account of the event:

"Ty Cobb was in the city yesterday from 9:30 o'clock in the morning until 11:30 last night when he and his bride left for Detroit. Everyone was expecting Tyrus on the 7:15 Georgia train from Atlanta and quite an aggregation of the fans were out bright and early to meet the train. However he failed to come, and there was considerable speculation as to his whereabouts. The idea was suggested that Cobb might have alighted from the train at Belair and driven across the country to the Lombard home.

"However, at 9:30 o'clock Ty, accompanied by his uncle, Mr. A. C. Ginn, reached here over the C&WC [railroad] and at once repaired to the room of Mr. William Sheron [located in downtown Augusta on Broad Street], where the famous Georgian dressed. An automobile was secured and made lightning quick time to the scene of the wedding. The trip was made in 25 minutes over good roads and one minute of twelve the groom and his party arrived at the residence.

"Cobb is looking exceedingly well. He says that he is feeling splendidly with the exception of a game knee that was hurt some time ago while he was sliding a base. He also has a large number of bruises on his body, but when asked if they did not prevent him from doing as well as he otherwise might. Ty dismissed the subject lightly saying that when a ball player winces at every little scratch he is not fit to play in anything else except a peanut league. Ty looks brown because of sunburn and he has the ruddy complexion indicating perfect health. He expects to join the team in Detroit Saturday."

Hamilton's article went on to discuss the Tigers prospects and Cobb's planned trip to Japan to investigate the possibility of taking the game there. The society page had a much briefer account of the nuptials with a headline saying, BEAUTIFUL MARRIAGE OF MISS LOMBARD AND MR. COBB, and with the article, also mostly likely written by Hamilton, reporting: "The ceremony which united the lives of Miss Charlie Lombard and Mr. Tyrus Cobb was sweetly solemnized yesterday at high noon at The Oaks, the beautiful country home of the bride. The home was charmingly decorated with palms, ferns and cut flowers. The affair throughout was marked by that simplicity which is the keynote of elegance. As Miss Lombard, Mrs. Cobb, enjoyed a wide popularity and her sweet face is but an index to her lovely disposition. Of Mr. Cobb, it is enough to say that he is the idol of the fans. Lucky in his chosen profession, he has carried that luck into the matrimonial world. And has been most fortunate in winning the heart of Miss Lombard."

Following the conclusion of the wedding, a buffet was offered the guests at which the new couple was toasted repeatedly and presented with several gifts, including a silver punch bowl from some of Cobb's local fans. The wedding principals and guests then journeyed to downtown Augusta where a supper party was given by the bride's parents at the Genesta Hotel on the corner of Jackson (Eighth) and Broad Streets, about a block from where Cobb refereed the wrestling match in the Grand Opera House.

Ty was twenty-one years old at the time of the wedding, and Charlie was eighteen. Cobb's uncle, Clifford Ginn, was the only person from Cobb's family to attend. And in spite of the rather extensive coverage the wedding received in the Augusta newspapers, the details given there raise many questions: Why in the world would Cobb want to ride all those long hours on trains to Augusta only to be there fifteen hours and get on another train to head back to Detroit with his new bride? Why didn't they just wait a month or so until the baseball season would be over, and they could leave immediately on a honeymoon trip? Why didn't they have an elaborate church wedding since Charlie came from such a prominent family? And why was the only wedding party member or guest from Cobb's side of the family his uncle, Clifford Ginn?

The answers to these questions are lost to time since all members of the wedding party are now deceased. The important thing is that a young man from northeastern Georgia and a young woman from the middle of the state made a commitment to share each other's lives and start their own family.

And that's exactly what they did.

# PRESS SCRUTINY AND BROTHER PAUL        7

"TYRUS," A FRIEND ASKED COBB, "how does it feel to have yourself talked about in every Southern city, to have cartoonists draw your picture, to have the *Sporting Life* devote half a page of reciting your doings on American League diamonds?"

With hesitation Cobb replied, "Just the same as if they never mentioned my name."

That exchange was reported by the *Augusta Chronicle* on Halloween Day of 1907, when Cobb was only in his second full season in the major leagues. The reporter noted that Cobb was wearing a gold medal under his waistcoat presented to him for being the "heavy hitter" of the American League and additionally was carrying a watch Augusta fans had given him on his last day with the Tourists.

"He is a magnificent specimen of manhood," the writer glowingly observed. "Just about an even six feet, he stands erect as an Indian, deep-chested and with broad, square shoulders that fill his coat in a way to make any tailor proud to fit his figure. He is not as fleshy as he was when here last winter, but his muscles are hard as nails, and he shows the affect of a good manager's training, aided and abetted by the fact that he is strictly temperate, and as steady in his habits of living as many a man of double his years."

That *Chronicle* reporter's observations were typical of how the Fourth Estate treated Cobb with in-depth reporting of both his public and private happenings. His hometown newspapers, the *Augusta Chronicle* and *Augusta Herald*, loved to brag about Cobb when he was doing great, but they also wrote about when he was in a slump or when he was involved in physical altercations on and off the field.

National writers and famous people of the day often came to see him and his family as they divided their early years living in Detroit during the baseball season and spending their time mostly in Royston or Augusta in off-seasons. Before the Cobbs found a home of their own, their Augusta home base was The Oaks, home of Charlie's parents.

On November 10, 1908, just three months after Charlie and Ty's marriage, the *Chronicle* reported, "Looking in the very best of condition, Ty Cobb came to the city [Augusta] yesterday and spent several hours here. He and Mrs. Cobb are spending time with Mr. and Mrs. R. O. Lombard, the parents of Mrs. Cobb who live nine miles in the country.

"Ty says that he is thoroughly rested from the hard work he did in the world's series and is now hunting ducks and quail as a means of diversion."

Cobb was further quoted as saying about his first day of hunting back in Augusta, "I shot four ducks down with my repeating gun while they were flying and I killed two others on the water with one discharge of the gun." He added, "Think I would like hunting in this neck of the woods as a winter's recreation."

Eleven days later, the *Chronicle* again was reporting on another of Cobb's hunting trips, this time taken with his nineteen-year-old brother, Paul; his father-in-law, Roswell Lombard; the police chief of Augusta, M. J. Norris; and another friend, Walter Kent. The group boarded a boat called *The Swan* for a trip down the Savannah River to a hunting area 150 miles below Augusta.

The *Chronicle* also told its readers about Cobb's younger brother. "Paul Cobb is a brilliant young athlete whom [Manager] Jimmy McAleer of the St. Louis Browns drafted from Joplin, Missouri. Paul hit near the .350 mark and is considered as promising as his wonderful brother was at the same age. Paul is only 19 years of age and looks even younger. He is about as tall as Ty is, but is not so heavy and he resembles his 'big bud' in many particulars.

Paul is expected to be a bright and shining star in the American League within a year or two."

Like his brother, Paul Cobb had made a strong impression playing on the local amateur team in Royston. He then landed a spot on the Kalamazoo team of the Michigan State League pitching and playing outfield. He next went to Joplin, Missouri, in the Western Association where he played 140 games, batted .373, and stole 34 bases.

As the year came to a close, Ty Cobb marked his twenty-second birthday on December 18, 1908. On December 27, the *Chronicle* reported that Ted Sullivan "probably the most famous baseball manager and scout in the country" had sent a letter to the *Sporting News* magazine proclaiming Cobb to be "the grandest ball player today in the national game."

Sullivan specifically noted, "When I saw Ty Cobb play last year, I was more than pleased to discover that Dixie has at last produced a base ball player that equals the best of the past in the two great essentials of the game—batting and base running.

"Base running is the spectacular part of the game," Sullivan continued, "yet it is the essential and culminating element in winning games. There never was a great champion club in a major league that did have five or six magnetic fleet base runners on it."

In February of 1909, the *Chronicle* turned its focus on Ty's brother, Paul, and his future with the St. Louis Browns of the American League. But two months later the paper was telling readers that Paul just might show up in Augusta wearing the uniform of his brother's former team, the Augusta Tourists!

"Some days ago a friend of Paul Cobb in Augusta received a letter from him stating that he would like to play here, and the local club owners then took the matter up with Jim McAleer, manager of the St. Louis team," the *Chronicle* reported on April 27. "The result was that McAleer placed a rather steep price on Cobb's release, but negotiations are still underway, and it is possible that the brother to the now famous American League baseman will shine on the same diamond that Ty did four years ago."

Even though the Tourists had not yet completed any arrangements with the St. Louis baseball club, Paul Cobb indeed was a guest player with the

Tourists on April 29, 1909, for a game against the Palmettos team from Columbia, South Carolina.

The day of the match at Warren Park, the *Chronicle* observed of Paul's appearance, "He is expected to prove a big drawing card for there are hundreds of Augusta fans who want to see him in action on the battle grounds where Ty first gave promise of becoming a world-famous athlete."

As it turned out, only a "fair sized crowd" showed up for the game, but those who did were treated to see the Tourists shut out the Palmettos, 3–0. The *Chronicle* noted, "Paul Cobb appeared in right field and made a splendid showing. He was at the bat three times and secured one hit, driving the ball to left for a clean single."

The next week Paul Cobb was back in a Tourists uniform playing right field, replacing Cadawalder Coles who had a sprained ankle. The Tourists were in Columbus, Georgia, preparing to play the team there when Tourists manager Louis Castro wired Augusta Tourists baseball club secretary J. S. Farr of the need to substitute Cobb for Coles. *Chronicle* sports editor Hamilton reported, "It is earnestly hoped by local fandom that the Augusta and St. Louis managements can come to an agreement regarding Cobb's release to Augusta throughout the present season. Cobb is anxious to play with Augusta and Augusta fans are anxious for him to play. He is a coming ball player and will be a star in this [SALLY] League."

Unfortunately, the two games that Paul Cobb played right field in Columbus, Georgia, wearing the Augusta Tourists uniform were not his best. He came up to bat four times in each of the games on Tuesday, May 4, and Wednesday, May 5, but made no hits and subsequently scored no runs. But while his brother struggled on field, Ty Cobb's reputation continued to grow in 1909 both in positive and negative ways.

In a photograph taken on August 24, 1909, when the Tigers played and beat the Philadelphia Athletics, 7–6, in a closely fought game, Cobb came flying into third base with his right leg high the air and caught Athletics third baseman Frank Baker on the arm. The incident reportedly led American League president Ban Johnson to threaten that Cobb must stop that sort of playing or else he would have to quit the game.[12]

Sometime after the Baker incident, Cobb was quoted in the *Chronicle*, on January 20, 1910, from a letter he wrote to league president Johnson.

"I want to say there is a good way to eliminate accidents caused by spikes," Cobb wrote, "that is to make a rule for every man in the American League to file his spikes off to where they are commenced to sharpen, which is done at the factory, and the umpire can examine the ball players' shoes before every game, as that could be done when each team is idle, while the opposing team practices as they are required to occupy the bench at that time.

"I suggest this as I have been wrongfully and severely censured by many of the press representatives and public, and, to be truthful, I never spiked a man willingly, and I would feel grateful if you would present my motion in some official form. I feel that I should do something to place myself right with the people who believe me to be a rowdy and blackguard.

"When I go on the field next year, I will always be afraid of spiking someone, as I was after the last Philadelphia game, as any of the Boston or Detroit players will testify.

"Wishing you a pleasant winter, etc., and kind personal regards, I hope to remain, as ever, Ty Cobb."

Ty ended the major-league season with a batting average of .377. He had played in 156 games, with 573 at bats, had 216 hits and 116 runs, hitting 9 home runs. He also managed to rack up an amazing 76 stolen bases!

But the season ended with a major incident that would color the rest of Cobb's career.

The Tourists lost the first of the two games, 2–1, and lost the second game, 2–0. When the Tourists played the Charleston (South Carolina) Sea Gulls on Thursday, May 6, in Charleston, Cadawalder Coles was back playing right field and Paul Cobb was not in the lineup.

While Paul Cobb was trying to establish his own place in the game, on September 7, a warrant charging his brother with "assault with intent to kill" was sworn out before Cleveland, Ohio, justice William Brown by J. J. Klein, attorney for George Stanfield, a black night watchman at the Euclid

---

12 Cobb flying high with his spiked shoes in the air is how his statue at Turner Stadium in Atlanta depicts him.

Hotel in Cleveland. Stanfield contended that Cobb had returned late to his hotel room and became confused as to which room was his. Stanfield further contended when he tried to set Cobb straight on which room was his, Cobb got angry and pulled a knife on the watchman.

On November 22, Cobb returned to Cleveland to answer the charge. He pled guilty in criminal court on a lesser charge of assault and battery that did away with the necessity of a trial, and he was fined $100 and court costs.

The ugly incident apparently did not bother U.S. president William Howard Taft[13] who hooked up with Cobb at the Augusta Country Club on Milledge Road just two months after the alleged Cleveland assault happened. Taft, in fact, was eager to meet with Cobb when he learned that the baseball player was at his Augusta home a short distance from the country club where Taft was to play golf. The *Chronicle* reported the president and the ballplayer did meet about 11:00 a.m. on November 8, 1909, and for fifteen to twenty minutes shared "a very pleasant conversation."

The *Chronicle*'s coverage was headlined, PRESIDENT TAFT GREETS TY COBB, BALL PLAYER, and quoted Taft as saying, "I am very glad to see you, Mr. Cobb, probably I should say 'Ty.' I am glad to again meet the most popular Georgian and, if I may say it, the most distinguished Augustan."

According to the *Chronicle*, "The intimacy between the President and Ty Cobb originated through Charlie Taft, the President's son. Charlie is a great admirer of Cobb and, when the ball player was in Washington recently, he insisted that Cobb call on his father. The result was that the entire Detroit club were visitors at the White House, and it will be recalled that at that time the President greeted Cobb as his 'fellow citizen of Augusta, Georgia.'

"While President Taft personally is a follower of golf," the *Chronicle* article continued, "he extols the sensational game of baseball. As he said to Cobb yesterday, 'Baseball is the game for young Americans. Golf is a better game for older Americans.'"

---

13 Taft loved three of the same outdoor pursuits Ty Cobb loved: baseball, golf, and automobiles. Taft is said to be the first U.S. president to enjoy golf as a hobby. He was the first to own an automobile and in 1909 converted the White House stables into a four-car garage. And, most importantly to baseball fans, he was the first U.S. president to throw out the first ball of a new baseball season, on April 14, 1910, at League Park in Baltimore, Maryland, when he threw a ball to future Hall of Famer Walter Johnson of the Washington Senators before the start of a game between the Senators and the Philadelphia Athletics.

Another national celebrity who wanted to be seen with Cobb at the close of 1909 was a vaudeville minstrel show comedian named George "Honey Boy" Evans. He was wearing blackface (burnt-cork makeup) on the stage of Augusta's Grand Opera House on December 28, between the first and second acts of his show, when he presented Cobb with a huge, silver trophy "for being the champion batsman of the world."

The trophy was reported to be four feet tall and to have cost Evans $1,000. Cobb would display it in the living room of his house near the foot of the main staircase leading to the second floor.

Evans called prominent Augusta attorney C. Henry Cohen to the stage. It was Cohen who actually handed Cobb the trophy saying, "Fitting it is that the state of his nativity and this, the county of his adoption, should be selected as the place of crowning Tyrus Cobb the king of base ball players for the year 1909, and, as I crown him King Tyrus the First, I can hear the 50 million fans of the United States with one acclaim crying, 'Long live the King.'"

In accepting the trophy amid a storm of applause, the *Chronicle* quoted Cobb as saying that he "had a splendid opportunity to show the people of Augusta just how poor a speaker he was when he tried to express his appreciation to Mr. Evans for the magnificent trophy."

The *Chronicle* concluded: "As Ty finished his response and was retiring from the stage, the band struck up "Dixie" and the audience almost went wild. A Southern boy, a Georgia boy, an Augusta boy had received a token crowning him king in his profession and not an individual left the Opera House who was not proud of the South, of Georgia and of Ty Cobb."

Ty apparently expected his earning power to continue unabated because by the end of 1909 he was investing his money in land. The *Augusta Chronicle* on December 29 told readers that the *Hazlehurst News* had reported that Cobb had bought three thousand acres in the southern part of Jeff Davis County, paying $20,000 for it. "He was down here last winter looking around and while here bought a nice little farm two miles from town and had a pretty little cottage erected on it," the *Hazlehurst News* reported. "And he also purchased some residence lots in the town of Hazlehurst. And now by investing $20,000 in Jeff Davis county dirt, proves conclusively that he is a good business man as well as a great ball player.

"Ty Cobb has had enough nice things said about him by the press in all parts of the country for his head to be as big as a flour barrel," the small-town newspaper reported, "but it hasn't affected him as a ball player. While down here last winter prospecting he was in our office two or three times and, if he had any swell head about him, we failed to discover it. And this is one reason why he is so popular with the public. He stands at the head of the list as a ball player."

The *Chronicle* in April of 1910 in reporting Cobb leaving for spring training with the Detroit Tigers likewise echoed the *Hazlehurst News* in the belief that Cobb's success had not gone to his head. "Cobb is well admired in Augusta not wholly because he is the greatest baseball player in the history of the game but because he is a fine fellow, straightforward, plain as an old shoe, a devoted husband and a good citizen."

Cobb had another great season in 1910 beginning it with the birth of his first son and the first of his five children, Tyrus Raymond Cobb Jr., on January 30.

Cobb also would end his 1910 season on a happy note with a batting average of .385; even better than the previous year when "Honey Boy" Evans gave him the trophy. He had played in 140 games, batted 509 times, had 196 hits, including 8 home runs, and scored 106 runs. And he racked up another amazing 65 stolen bases!

Late November of 1910 found Cobb, the country boy from northern Georgia, playing a series of exhibition games with the Detroit Tigers in Havana, Cuba. He would tell *Chronicle* reporters on returning to Augusta for the off-season that Eugenio Jiménez is "the moving spirit of baseball" on the island and that Jiménez had labored twelve hard years to bring baseball into prominence in Cuba.

Cobb especially noted the financial difficulties in playing baseball in Cuba. As the *Chronicle* reported: "The rent paid for the ground on which they play, all improvements provided by the club, is $12,000 per year, and it is the only suitable field in this city of 360,000 inhabitants. Salaries can be estimated by the salary paid the ground keeper, $125 per month. Police protection costs $350 monthly, and the expense of importing the Detroit and Philadelphia teams for a series was approximately $40,000. Considering the fact that the diamond is so sandy that the play is very slow, this is a great undertaking."

Nevertheless with all the obstacles, Cobb predicted that Cuba would be the sporting center of the world in the next two years.

By early March of 1911, Cobb was ready to join the Detroit Tigers at their spring training site in Monroe, Louisiana. The *Chronicle* staff had a great time with the story about Cobb heading for spring training with his growing family that now included his son, with the unknown editor coming up with this headline, TY, MRS. TY AND TY JR. LEAVE HOME TODAY. Cobb and his family headed off by automobile to his former hometown of Royston before driving to Atlanta where his car and his family would get on a train and ride the rails to Louisiana.

The 1911 season would find Cobb racking up the first of three batting averages above .400, with his first being his best, .420. He would also bat better than .400 in 1912 (.410) and 1922 season (.401).

Cobb also would end his 1911 season having played in 146 games, coming to bat 591 times, with 248 hits, including eight home runs, and scoring 147 runs. And he racked up another amazing 83 stolen bases, his second best in that endeavor. (His best season for stolen bases would be 1915 with 96 steals.)

His expertise on the diamonds was such that on October 17, at the Polo Grounds in New York City, before the start of the 1911 World Series, he was presented with a new automobile. It was awarded to him by a commission of baseball writers as the player of either the American or National League "who had been of the greatest assistance to his team during the season."

The following month Cobb would have another memorable experience in crossing paths in Augusta with Thomas Woodrow Wilson who stopped over in Augusta on November 18, to visit old friends and scenes of his childhood while heading for a vacation in St. Augustine, Florida. He then was governor of New Jersey after serving as president of Princeton University and was preparing to run for president in 1912.

Wilson had lived in Augusta a half century before Cobb, while his father was pastor of the downtown area First Presbyterian Church at Greene and Seventh Streets. Wilson would say his earliest memory in Augusta was when

## Major-League Batting Champion

Cobb's batting record in the major leagues had begun with his first hit at his very first time at bat in the major leagues on August 30, 1905, playing for the Tigers. That was a double off Jack Chesbro of the New York Yankees, and it drove in two runs.

He went into the start of the 1911 season with 960 hits under his belt, racking up his 1,000th a few weeks later. And he began his 1916 season with 1,937 hits, racking up his 2,000th shortly afterward when he was only twenty-nine years old.

To put that in perspective, New York Yankees third baseman Álex Rodríguez on July 21, 2006, recorded his 2,000th career hit, which made him only the eighth player to record that number before his thirty-first birthday. The only others (at this writing) to reach the 2,000-hit mark before their thirty-first birthday are Rogers Hornsby (age 29), Mel Ott (30), Hank Aaron (30), Joe Medwick (30), Jimmie Foxx (30), Robin Yount (30), and, of course, Ty Cobb (29).

Cobb's 3,000th hit had come on August 19, 1921, off Elmer Meyers of the Red Sox in the second game of a doubleheader. It had taken Cobb sixteen years from his major league debut to reach this mark, and another six years before he would get his amazing 4,000th.

As of 2006, there were only twenty-six major-league players to be members of the 3,000-hit club with the top ten being: Pete Rose, 4,256; Ty Cobb, 4,189; Hank Aaron, 3,771; Stan Musial, 3,630; Cobb's good friend Tris Speaker, 3,514; Carl Yastrzemski, 3,419; Cap Anson, 3,418; Honus Wagner, 3,415; Paul Molitor, 3,319; and Eddie Collins, 3,315.

In writing about 4,000 hits by major leaguers, it should be noted historians also cite Theodore Roosevelt "Double Duty" Radcliffe of the Negro Leagues, who was said to have played for more than thirty teams, have more than 4,000 hits, and more than 400 home runs. He died on August 11, 2005, at the age of 103.

he was four, hearing people say Abraham Lincoln had been elected president and there would be war.

Wilson arrived in Augusta on November 18, 1911, shortly before noon on the Southeastern Limited of the Southern Railway and was taken on a two-hour driving tour around the city. He then checked into the Albion Hotel on Broad Street and took off walking around downtown Augusta. The *Chronicle* would later report, "He said he wanted to go alone and look over the city and visit the places he had not seen for many years and note the changes that have taken place since the time he went away [almost] as a 14-year-old lad."

Wilson was back at his hotel by 6:00 p.m. where he met with old friends and prominent local citizens for an hour, including Ty Cobb. The *Chronicle* related that, "an interesting feature at this reception was the introduction of Ty Cobb to the distinguished son of Augusta. 'How do you do, Mr. Cobb?' exclaimed Governor Wilson as soon as he heard the name, and the two shook hands warmly. 'I had the pleasure of meeting you in Atlanta last year, governor,' said Ty. 'Yes,' answered the governor, 'and I hope I will meet you often again.' Ty then told him of the victory of Princeton over Yale in the football game earlier in the afternoon and the former Princeton president was much pleased and said so."

Following the Albion Hotel reception, Governor Wilson went to the home of Bowdre Phinizy,[14] editor of the *Augusta Herald*, to have dinner. Wilson then went from his private dinner to the Grand Opera House at Eighth and Greene Streets, where he would see Ty Cobb play a football hero named Billy Bolton in the George Ade's comedy, *The College Widow*.

The day after Cobb's encounter with Wilson, on the evening of Sunday, November 19, the Augusta Press Club held a "roast" for Cobb in the Albion Hotel, with members of the local press and several of Cobb's close friends in attendance. The hotel was the same one in which he had resided as a young ballplayer with the Augusta Tourists.

"Ty Cobb has furnished many a line of 'copy' for all of the newspapers," the *Chronicle* related the next day. "He is a wonderful man, and he was told

---

14 Phinizy had been a student of Wilson's at Princeton.

face to face of his qualities last night for he was the guest of the Augusta Press Club.

"Ty was made to feel perfectly at home for this is his home, and he realized the strong bond of fellowship that exists between him and all Augustans. Ty said that he was overjoyed. He is modest but last night he threw away his modesty and had a heart to heart talk with his friends."

Later in the article the *Chronicle* related, "He was griddled, and he liked it. Of course, all the old baseball jokes were rung in and some were hits and some were kicks (all of the same being baseball terms). The food was excellent, the good cheer was contagious and everybody went home happy to have spent an evening with Ty Cobb, the world's greatest baseball player. It might be mentioned that Cobb was elected a life member of the club unanimously."

There were many, many times that Cobb was glad to get back home to Augusta, and such was the case with the events of Thursday, May 15, during the 1912 baseball season. The Detroit Tigers were on their way to beating the New York Highlanders three out of four games on the Highlanders' home turf, when—just as Detroit was up at bat in the fourth inning—Cobb jumped into the grandstand and beat the hell out of a spectator who had been taunting him with what others later testified to be racial remarks, including calling him a "half-nigger." The spectator turned out to be Claude Lueker, a former pressman, who had lost one hand and most of the other in a printing-press accident.

Lueker's account of the incident, which was printed in the edition of the *Chronicle*, follows:

"I was sitting with some friends just back of third base. When the Detroit team came on the field, there was a good deal of kidding and booing of Cobb. I did not hear any one make a remark that was out of the way. It all seemed good natured. I had on an alpaca coat, and Cobb seemed to single me out for he yelled back, 'Oh, go back to your waiter's job.'

"The yelling at Cobb kept up. We could see that he was getting excited. Somebody shouted an unpleasant characterization at him. Then he came straight for me followed by half a dozen players with bats in their hands. He hit me in the face with his fist, knocked me over, jumped on me, kicked me, spiked me and booted me behind the ear.

"When it was over some of my friends wanted me to have him arrested, but I did not want that done. He probably would have gotten off with a light fine."

Cobb's version of the event was much different, but he did express regret for hitting the spectator. He contended that Leuker was the aggressor and the same man had annoyed him on other occasions. "Yesterday, I tried to avoid the man but when his language became too much for me to stand, I lost my head," he said.

Cobb immediately was put out of the game by the umpire and was subsequently suspended indefinitely from playing baseball by American League president Ban Johnson.

The *New York Sun* would report, "Spectators in the vicinity said the man had been giving Cobb a verbal grilling for some time, that he had been warned to keep still and that his language was decidedly personal and offensive. The man said, according to one report, that he had guyed Cobb for fumbling a grounder and the latter had made a coarse and personal retort."

Other New York press said that after the incident, Detroit manager Hughie Jennings went over to the press stand and explained the fan had called Cobb "a half-nigger." Jennings supposedly told press members that "no Southerner would stand such an insult."

He added, "I heard the remark, but I knew it would be useless to restrain Ty as he would have got his tormentor sooner or later. When Ty's Southern blood is aroused, he is a bad man to handle."

Cobb complained of his suspension, "Johnson has always believed himself to be infallible. He suspends a man first and then investigates afterward. It should be the reverse."

Johnson was unmoved by Cobb's offer of apology. He replied, "Cobb's suspension stands until the matter is fully investigated. . . . Speaking of the case unofficially, it looks as if Cobb went way wrong in his actions. Of course, he may have had great provocation. The fellow may have abused him just as Cobb claims he did—but where are the rules and what are they for? Cobb had but to appeal to the umpire. The umpire upon Cobb's request would have had no option, he would have had the rooter thrown out of the ball park and that would have been the end of the affair. What right did Cobb have to rush into the stand, knock down a man and kick him with his spikes?"

After the suspension, Cobb's Detroit teammates the next day refused to play another game until Cobb was reinstated. Eighteen members of the Tigers organization signed a statement that was sent to American League President Johnson: "Feeling Mr. Cobb is being done an injustice by your action in suspending him, we, the undersigned, refuse to play another game after today until such action is adjusted to our satisfaction, as no one could stand such personal abuse from any one," the statement said. "We want him reinstated for tomorrow's game, May 18, or there will be no game. If players cannot have protection, we must protect ourselves."

Tigers manager Hughie Jennings said of the stand by his players: "The suspension was not warranted. I am in the hands of my friends. If they refuse to play, I will finish away down in the league race. I expect Mr. Johnson to reconsider the matter, fine Cobb or announce definitely the length of Cobb's suspension."

Jennings did manage to round up some substitute players to play the Philadelphia Americans the next day and keep from being subjected to more sanctions from President Johnson. And, as might be expected, Philadelphia beat the substituted Detroit players, 24–2.

The American League presidents in a special meeting on May 21 fined each member of the Detroit team who signed the protest statement $100 for refusing to play ball in Philadelphia on the previous Saturday and Monday. However, the Tigers club president, Frank J. Navin, promised to pay his players' fines for their protest action if they would return to the field, and the club presidents decided as a group to take steps to have their baseball grounds better policed and take any actions to prevent a reoccurrence of what had happened in New York. That would include advising players that, if attacked by a spectator, verbally or otherwise, they had the right to appeal to the umpire for protection.

On May 25, Ban Johnson announced Cobb's reinstatement and ordered, in addition to his ten days suspension already served, Cobb to pay a fine of $50. The next day Cobb was back on the team with the Detroit Tigers in

Chicago, and the Tigers celebrated the return of their star player by beating the White Sox, 6–2.

Cobb ended the 1912 season with his second-best season batting average: .410. He had played in 140 games, been at bat 553 times, had 227 hits, and scored 119 runs, while hitting 7 home runs. And he racked up another amazing 61 stolen bases.

While Ty was having another great season, his brother was having a rough one.

"Paul Cobb, right fielder of the Lincoln Western League team and a brother of Tyrus Cobb is out of the game for the season with a broken arm sustained in the fourth inning of the first game with Des Moines yesterday," the *Chronicle* reported on September 12, 1912. "He was hit by a pitched ball."

It wasn't easy being Ty Cobb's brother.

# LIFE ON WILLIAMS STREET                                   8

In April 1913, a two-story home just off Walton Way near what is now the main entrance to Augusta State University became the place where Cobb and his wife would raise their children, where he welcomed nationally famous visitors, where he would hold press conferences, and where he truly felt safe at home.

The Cobb family was growing. Ty Jr.'s birth was announced in the *Augusta Chronicle* on February 1, 1910, with a two-paragraph story headlined, LATEST DIAMOND PROSPECT TYRUS RAYMOND COBB JR. Besides Ty Jr. and Beverly, three other children would be born into the Cobb family: Shirley, the oldest daughter and the only one of the five children to be born in Detroit; Herschel, obviously named after Cobb's father's father; and, finally, Jimmy.

As a major leaguer, Cobb had continued to spend spring training in Augusta, and the month before he bought his Augusta house, Cobb pulled together a team of Georgians, including members of the Augusta Tourists and Royston Reds, to take on the Brooklyn Superbas in Augusta for spring training. Cobb's collection of players met on March 24, at Warren Park in Augusta. The *Chronicle*'s headline that day ran, BIG LEAGUE BALL PLAYERS TO BATTLE FOR BLOOD WITH COBB.

Apparently to get his team in shape for the Brooklyn game, Cobb took his players on the road to Athens, Georgia, where on March 22, 1913,

Cobb and "a bunch he has gathered together in and around Royston" played the University of Georgia team on Sanford Field and defeated the collegians, 5–2. "Cobb played in his old place [center field], Tommy Mc-Millan of Brooklyn was on short, Ducky Holmes of Augusta pitched, being relieved for part of the game by Rheney," the *Chronicle* later reported of the Athens game. "Gonzalez[15] of the Boston Nationals caught for the visitors. Cobb himself got only one hit out of four times at bat. Corley for the collegians pitched a good ball and hit a three-bagger for the two runs which the Red and Black scored."

Although Cobb's team managed to beat the University of Georgia team, their luck ran out when facing the Brooklyn Superbas on March 24, back in Augusta just two days later. The match ended with Brooklyn beating Cobb's players, 7–1.

"Ty Cobb's team of Georgians went down in defeat in the sixth inning of the game played at Warren Park yesterday afternoon, when the Brooklyn swatters hammered the offerings of 'Ducky' Holmes to all corners, scoring four runs in this frame, after having been held to one hit in four innings by [former Augusta Tourists] Nap Rucker," the *Chronicle* reported the next day.

Cobb played first base instead of center field during the game with the *Chronicle* writing with glee, "All predictions of Cobb's ability were fulfilled yesterday when he treated the fans and fanabelles to a first-class exhibition of cavorting around the initial station. Two solid safeties were driven out by him in his four trips to the platter. His speed on the bases was marveled at by the crowds in the stands."

Overall, observed the *Chronicle,* "It was a great game and everybody went home satisfied, after seeing some of the greatest players the game has produced in action."[16]

---

15 González was Miguel Angel González, 6 foot 1, 200-pound native of Havana who had made his major league debut with the Boston Braves of the National League the year before in September of 1912. He became the third Cuban to play in the major leagues and the first Cuban to manage a major-league team (St. Louis Cardinals, 1938 and 1940).

16 The Brooklyn lineup, including substitutes, was Herbie Moran, right field; Leo Callahan, right field; George Cutshaw, second base; Zack Wheat, left field; Jake Daubert, first base; Red Smith. third base; Bob Fisher, shortstop; Otto Miller, catcher; Tex Erwin, catcher; Frank Allen, pitcher; Pat Ragan, pitcher; and the soon-to-be-immortal Casey Stengel playing center field

Cobb's ties to former Augusta resident Woodrow Wilson were renewed when Cobb visited the U.S. president in the White House on July 31, 1913. The *Chronicle* noted that Cobb came with Samuel J. Tribble, a U.S. representative from Georgia, and that "President Wilson greeted him warmly." Cobb, the article continued, had invited the president to see one of the Detroit-Washington games, especially one coming up that Saturday when a special cup was to be presented to Walter Johnson. The president said he would try to attend.

Cobb failed to bat above .400 in his 1913 season as he had the previous two seasons, but he did end the season at .390. He had played in 122 games, was at bat 428 times, scoring 70 runs on 167 hits, including 4 home runs. He had 52 stolen bases.

The *Chronicle* wrote about Ty's homecoming on October, 16, 1913, saying, "Ty Cobb is back home. He arrived yesterday from New York over the Atlantic Coast Line. Mrs. Cobb, who has been in Augusta for several weeks, greeted him at the station. They went directly to their home on The Hill [the high Summerville residential area] and so glad to get home once more was Cobb that he remained home the rest of the day, except for a short run down into the heart of town, where there were more and very enthusiastic greetings of a sort that must have warmed the cockles of his heart. Everybody's glad to see Ty back again."

Two days after Cobb returned to Augusta, he joined Judge Henry C. Hammond and Solicitor General A. L. Franklin at the annual banquet of the YMCA held on October 17, in the YMCA gymnasium with about 125 men in attendance. Cobb spoke about the organization's work, saying "that he could readily see the increased enthusiasm now over last year."

It didn't take long for Cobb to quickly fall into his off-season life in Augusta of visiting his friends, taking part in community activities, and spending time with his family. There always was a lot of activity in the Cobb house on Williams Street with the coming and going of the children's friends, Charlie's church and social friends, and Ty's friends and business associates.

Not all were happy days for the Cobb children, especially in the off-season winter months when their father was not on the road playing games.

His legendary temper wasn't limited to the baseball field; at home he'd beat his wife and children. "I never spent five seconds with that man that I wasn't scared pea green," his older daughter, Shirley, said. "He beat everybody, and we weren't bad children. I was always an A student, and he never once told me that was pretty good. I played Portia in the *Merchant of Venice* at the senior play at Bradford [Massachusetts] College. He came to see it, and his first remark to me was, 'You were out of character in such and such a scene and in this place.' But I was proud of what I had done. I had gotten up on a stage in front of him and others, and I didn't make any mistakes!"

Before she died, Cobb's youngest daughter, Beverly McLaren, would tell this author, "There always was a cook and a yard boy, and my brother, Jimmy, and I had a nurse for a while. My mother was a homebody. She loved her garden. She did belong to the Eastern Star. My mother was a Methodist, my father was a Baptist and we children went to [nearby] Reid Memorial Presbyterian Church on Walton Way. I never saw my father in church, but he wanted us to go. Mother was a church-goer but not regularly.

"We were raised in very lovely surroundings. Our homes [in Detroit and Augusta] were in good neighborhoods.[17] We went to the best schools, and we were taught the value of a dollar. I earned my allowance by washing my father's socks. I got three cents for the short ones and five cents for the long ones like he used for sports.

"We had a lot of animals at the Williams Street house. My sister had a show horse, my brother, Jimmy, had a Shetland pony. We had a billy goat. My brother, Herschel, also had a nanny goat. My father had fifteen hunting dogs in a kennel there. My mother had a canary bird. We also had two pigeons that got loose in the house one time. My younger brother and I also had rabbits. The canary moved west with us, and my sister's show horse came later.

"When I look back on Augusta, overall it was a happy living," Mrs. McLaren said. "We went swimming in the summer at Lombard's mill pond. That was not the commercial Lombard's Pond, but the pond where our grandparents lived."

---

17 During the summer months, the family joined their father in Detroit living in various houses on Commonwealth Avenue, LaSalle Boulevard, Third Avenue, Seminole Avenue, and in Grosse Pointe.

She also remembered her father's office in the house was a small room on the ground floor down the hall from the front entrance. There he kept his guns locked away and he had a rolltop desk.

"My father collected metal tobacco tags off plugs, and my mother had them pounded into the top of a table," Mrs. McLaren recalled. "I gave the table to the Ty Cobb Memorial in Royston along with a leather chair he used and some oriental things. I kept a barrel of his canceled checks and gave them away for a while to people who wanted his autograph. Now I charge for them and give the money to his educational foundation. My husband suggested I do that."

She also remembered occasionally standing up to her father when she was in college. "My father used to say to us children, 'Who gave you the right to think?' I was a sophomore at college, and he asked me to come home and host a foursome at dinner. They were talking about Roosevelt, and I made a comment. He said, 'Who gave you the right to think?' and I replied, 'God gave me a brain, and you spent a lot of money developing it, and I hope you both haven't been failures.' He never said that to me again.

"When my future husband asked for his approval of our marriage, my father told him, 'Let me give you a word of advice. She has a mind like a steel trap, and don't get caught in it.'"

Cobb's oldest daughter, Shirley Beckworth, told this author her father always was a voracious reader and commented, "I never saw his light off in his bedroom. His light was always on, and he was always reading. He especially loved books about Napoleon and Julius Caesar."

When she was asked, "Didn't the bedroom light keep her mother awake?" Mrs. Beckworth replied, "They didn't sleep in the same room. He slept in the front room upstairs, and to the right of his room was the sewing room. Ty Jr. and I slept in the middle room. There was only eighteen months between us. As we got older, we slept in different rooms. My mother and the baby [Jimmy] were in the last bedroom."

In response to Mrs. Beckworth's revealing that her parents slept in separate bedrooms, the author of this book couldn't help remarking, "I suppose Ty and Charlie did sleep together since they had five kids." To which Mrs. Beckworth replied, "We always knew what was going on. My grandmother—his mother—said all Ty had to do was hang his trousers in the bedroom and Charlie would get pregnant. There were five children and eight miscarriages. She wasn't supposed to have any children after me. All of us were born at home except Jimmy [the youngest], and he was born in an Augusta hospital."

Mrs. Beckworth felt he really "didn't have time for his children."

She said, with emotion, "Any great person—and I don't care whether they are a genius or not—should not have any children. You're getting into a touchy area. I don't think he knew how to be around his children. And I don't think there ever will be a book written about Ty Cobb that will truly show him for what he really was. He was a very complex man. He was sentimental and soft for a sucker for everyone but his own children, and yet he wanted his children to excel. He never complimented me, so he must have been unhappy with me."

Was Cobb just as strict with all of his children? According to Mrs. Beckworth, "Mostly with Ty [Jr.] and me. We were the oldest. My brother always said we should all have been in an insane asylum. If I hadn't had my books and my music, I don't know what I would have done."

Mrs. Beckworth said she'd come to know her father better after he'd died in 1961 than when he was alive, in part due to letters written from Cobb to her mother, while he was traveling with the team. While talking about those letters, Mrs. Beckworth started crying. "They were some of the sweetest and most tender letters I've ever read. I don't think all the bad he did was due to Ty Cobb. I defended my mother all of her life, but I think she too was somewhat responsible. I finally realized that what he wanted was honesty from everybody, but mostly from his own family. If you can't believe your wife and children, who can you believe? It was so many simple things he asked for that she didn't do. Like he would ask if she had checked on his laundry to make sure it had come back from the cleaners. She said yes, even though it hadn't. Do you know he didn't have any of his uniforms when he retired?"

But, on the other hand, Mrs. Beckworth had to say, "Mr. Cobb [she actually called him either Mr. Cobb or TRC] blamed my mother for the attitude of the children, but I also blame Mr. Cobb. There's an attitude that develops when you are raised in an atmosphere of fear."

When asked if she didn't think her father was a psychopath, sort of a Southern version of Dr. Jekyll and Mr. Hyde, Mrs. Beckworth responded without qualification, "Yes, I do. How could he have been so sweet to other people and not to his own family? Everything important we did had to be done on his birthday, December 18, or as close to it as possible. As a baseball player, he had a great record," Mrs. Beckworth added, "but as a man, as a husband and father, he didn't have much of a one."

Naturally, many of the telephone calls to the Cobb home on Williams Street were from sportswriters anxious to know the latest happenings of the world's greatest ball player. "I lost my trust for newspapermen when I was eleven or twelve," Mrs. Beckworth told me a bit hesitatingly. "I remember at the time of the baseball scandal [1926], my father told us, 'I'm going to Washington, D.C., but don't tell anyone.' One day a writer for the *Detroit News* called the house and asked where my father had gone. He said to me, 'I'll give you my word of honor that I won't use it in the paper.' So, I told the writer, and he put it in the newspaper [anyway]. I thought my father would come home mad, but all Mr. Cobb said to me was, 'You've learned about newspapermen.'"

When Cobb's youngest daughter, Beverly Cobb McLaren, was asked if her father tried to get her oldest brother to play professional baseball, she replied emphatically, "Absolutely not! That was one thing my father realized. Baseball at the time he started playing it was a very rough game. His own family did not like him playing baseball, and he was considered the black sheep of his family for doing so.

While his father was playing and managing for the Detroit Tigers and setting baseball records that would stand for decades, Ty Jr. was attending school in Augusta and trying to live as normal a life as possible. His key sports while attending the Academy of Richmond County on Walton Way were football and tennis. His mind was made up early he wasn't going to try and emulate his famous father.

In fact, in October of 1912 when a reporter for the *Chronicle* asked the nearly three-year-old Ty Jr. whether he intended to be a pitcher or a heavy-hitting outfielder like his dad, he was quoted as answering, "Naw, not gonna play ball." The boy knew early on that would be a big mistake, and probably by the age of three already was tired of having people ask if he was going to grow up to be like his father.

Her sister, Beverly, also observed, "There was no question in my mind that he loved us. He told us that. He would say, 'Because I love you, I'm doing what I'm doing.' . . . He was just a strong disciplinarian who demanded a great deal that young people don't understand. My mother believed in raising children one way, and my father believed in raising children another way. There was some friction, and the children got caught in between."

Ty Cobb's parenting style was revealed in an article F. C. Lane wrote for *The Baseball Magazine* in 1916. Cobb told Lane that he overheard Ty Jr., then about six, getting into an argument with another boy. Cobb said he felt his son wasn't standing up for his rights and warned him, "Now, that boy may be older than you but he is no bigger. He has insulted you, and, if you don't go out and lick him, I will lick you."[18]

Before Ty Jr. got out of high school, his parents already were having serious marital problems, and in 1931 Charlie Cobb moved her children out of the Williams Street house into a house at 1122 Greene Street. Ty Jr. attended Princeton University, where he played tennis and flunked out. He then attended Yale, where he captained the varsity tennis team. He started becoming his own man, which led to conflicts with his father. It was when Ty Jr. went to Yale the rift really deepened.

As Shirley Beckworth told it: "My father bought stock and put it in all of our children's names. Once over something, he got angry and sold all of Ty Jr.'s stock in General Motors. He especially got mad when Ty Jr. wouldn't come home one Christmas at his father's request."

Ty Jr. eventually settled down and graduated from the Medical College of South Carolina in Charleston, South Carolina, on June 4, 1942, and began his internship at University Hospital in Augusta the next month. The day before receiving his degree in Charleston, his mother joined him in Augusta and accompanied him to Charleston for the graduation. She returned to Augusta to visit her parents on Dean's Bridge Road.

---

18 It was no wonder Cobb's middle boy, Herschel, came to be regarded as the neighborhood bully.

One doctor who taught and remembered Ty Jr. in Augusta, Harry Pinson, recalled, "He called his father every name in the book. I knew that his father had cut off his medical school financial aid." (According to Ty Jr.'s teenage friend, Billy Calhoun, it was his father, Frank Calhoun, who loaned Ty Jr. the money to finish his medical school education.)

Ty Jr. met Mary Frances Dunn of Daytona Beach, Florida, through mutual friends while on a fishing trip to the Florida coast, and they married June 13, 1942, and took up housekeeping in Augusta at 2348 McDowell Street while he finished his internship.

The couple's first child, Tyrus Raymond Cobb III, was born in Augusta while his father was working on his internship. Besides his son, Ty Cobb III, who would die in 1984 at the age of forty-two, Ty Jr. and his wife had two other children: Charlie Marion Cobb, named after his Augusta-born paternal grandmother, and a daughter, Peggy Cobb Schug, who lives in Charlotte, North Carolina. "Daddy didn't want to deliver any of us, even though he delivered many, many babies," Charlie Cobb said.[19] "You know how superstitious some doctors are."

Before she died, Ty Jr.'s widow told this author her ten years of marriage to Ty Jr. were happy ones. Her husband enjoyed hunting and fishing and became a respected doctor in town. They even were visited in Dublin, Georgia, by Ty Jr.'s retired father. "The child of someone famous is a difficult position," the widow of Dr. Cobb said. "People always wanted to talk with him about his father. He was not reluctant to talk about his father when people asked, but he did not like to dwell on it."

Mrs. Cobb also said she understood why her father-in-law had been so tough on his children. "Cobb was superstrict, but I think that was partly because he wanted his kids to look good in life and wanted them to succeed," she said. "Ty Jr. had a volatile relationship with his father, but he still respected him. And people in Dublin liked Ty Jr. as a doctor and respected him."

---

19 Charlie Cobb lettered in football three years and basketball and baseball two years at Seabreeze High School in Daytona Beach, Florida, and was signed in June of 1963 to a football grant-in-aid at Georgia Tech in Atlanta. Seabreeze High Coach Fred Hogan said Charlie, at 6 feet 2 and weighing 185 pounds, "looks like his grandfather and he plays with some of that same determination."

On April 13, 1951, Herschel became the first of Ty Sr.'s five children to die, at age thirty-three. The following year, Ty Jr. was diagnosed with a brain tumor. He was operated on without success at the Neurological Institute in New York City in March before his family moved him to Palo Alto, California, where he lived his final months in the home shared by his mother and sister, Shirley Beckworth. "We brought Ty Jr. to our home from New York, where he had been operated on," Mrs. Beckworth recalled. "We knew Dublin was hot in the summertime, and that wouldn't be good for him to go back there. Ty looked the picture of health to the end, but he had cancer of the brain that ate at his memory. He could tell you something one minute and forget it the next.

"Mr. Cobb [Ty Sr.] came to see him," Mrs. Beckworth added. "One day, while I was there, Ty Jr. and Mr. Cobb were talking about dogs and hunting. I heard my father say, 'I'll give you one of those.' Ty Jr. momentarily forgot my father was even there. He turned away and said, 'Shirl, he will never give me anything.'

"TRC was stunned. He went over to the window and looked out. Then he walked out of the room, and he never came back again. He couldn't have done that any more than he could have said he was sorry."

Ty Cobb Jr. died September 9, 1952, at forty-two, and was entombed in a crypt near his brother Herschel at Alta Mesa Cemetery in Palo Alto.

Ty Jr.'s son Charlie, who has an American League All-Star Game gold pocket watch given to his famous grandfather, remembers spending one memorable week with Ty Sr. at his hunting lodge in Lake Tahoe, Nevada. "He was very kind to us grandchildren and took us out on his inboard boat," Cobb recalls. But one of Charlie Cobb's favorite memories is not of his legendary ball-playing grandfather but rather of his own father whom he barely knew yet who tried to give his children a lot more love than he himself got growing up.

"I don't care what time he came in from treating his patients or delivering babies—sometimes two or three in the morning—my father always would come into our bedrooms and give us a kiss," Cobb recalls. "I probably remember that more about him than anything else."

# Captain Cobb Reports for Service 9

As TY COBB CONTINUED TO GROW in fame and fortune, he also continued to expand his business interests beyond just large land investments.

Just two years after becoming a major leaguer, Cobb's image in September of 1907 appeared in advertisements endorsing Coca-Cola, which had been concocted by Atlanta pharmacist John S. Pemberton in 1886, the year Cobb was born. The advertisement partially quotes Cobb as saying, "On days when we are playing a double-header I always find that a drink of Coca-Cola between the games refreshes me to such an extent that I can start the second game feeling as if I had not been exercising at all, in spite of my exertions in the first."

Cobb not only drank the stuff, but, at the insistence of his friend, Coca-Cola owner Robert Woodruff, invested in its stock when it was $36 a share. Cobb and Woodruff often hunted together on Woodruff's plantation near Ichauway, Georgia. The soft drink stock would make Cobb millions. He later encouraged his family members and fellow ballplayers to buy into the company before it got really big.

In March of 1910, the Augusta newspapers carried advertisements showing a drawing of Cobb holding a bat and endorsing "Granulated Cut Plug Smoking Tobacco" made by the F. R. Penn Tobacco Company. The advertisement stated, "What Ty Cobb is to the baseball world, this tobacco

## TY THE TYCOON

Ty Cobb became known for his shrewd business dealings off the baseball field. In 1911, Cobb was listed among the seventy-two stockholders of a company purchasing the *Augusta Chronicle*. Other names on the stockholders list included many of Cobb's close friends and of George R. Lombard, his wife's uncle.

In addition to the high salary he commanded as a player, Cobb was one of the first professional athletes to lend his name and image (in exchange for compensation) to promote products. In 1912, Cobb was lending his famous name to endorse Lewis 66 Rye Whiskey. The ad featured a drawing of him standing by his bat with Cobb saying, "Away Above Everything."

In March of 1915, the *Chronicle* reported Cobb had joined with two other men to open a bank in nearby Thomson, Georgia. The *Chronicle* noted, "Application has been filed with the [Georgia] secretary of state for a charter for the City Bank of Thomson at Thomson, Ga., with a capitalization of $25,000. The application bears the signatures of J. T. Neal of Thomson, Tyrus Cobb of Augusta and L. G. Neal of Atlanta."

In 1916, Cobb was endorsing a health drink called Nuxated Iron. The advertisement created to look and read like a newspaper story said: "New York, N.Y.—When interviewed in his apartment at Bretton Hall, Ty Cobb said: 'Hundreds of people write to me to know how I train and what I do to keep up that force and vitality which enables me to play practically every day of the entire baseball season. They wonder why I can play a better game today than when I was a youngster.

"'The secret is keeping up the supply of iron in my blood— exactly what everyone else can do if they will.

"'At the beginning of the present season I was nervous and run down from a bad attack of tonsillitis but soon the papers began to state, "Ty Cobb has come back. He is hitting up the old stride." The secret was iron—Nuxated Iron filled me with renewed life.

"'Now they say I'm worth $50,000 a year to any baseball team, yet without plenty of iron in my blood I wouldn't be worth five cents.'"

is to the smoking world—PERFECTION. We had to agree to put up the best tobacco on earth before he would allow us to use his name. WE ARE DOING IT. Now on the market at 10 cents the package. TRY ONE."

Also in 1916, five years after his starring role in the play *The College Widow*, Cobb joined again with the play's producer Vaughan Glaser. The producer, another native Georgian, in 1916 had formed the Sunbeam Motion Picture Company, and he persuaded Cobb to take the starring role in the silent film *Somewhere in Georgia*, released in 1917. The film is said to be the first movie starring a major sports figure.

In spite of its title, *Somewhere in Georgia* was filmed over a two-week period in New York in the winter of 1916. It was directed by George Ridgwell and based on a story by Cobb's longtime friend, sportswriter Grantland Rice. Cobb reportedly was paid $10,000 up front for his acting services and name recognition. He acted the role of a Georgia bank clerk with a talent for baseball who gets hired by the Detroit Tigers. He is forced to leave behind his girlfriend, the banker's daughter, played by actress Elsie McLeod. Cobb comes back to the town to play an exhibition game, ends up beating up some bad guys who try to kidnap him, and recaptures the heart of the banker's daughter.

The movie, as might be expected, was a hit in small and midsize towns where baseball fans could not travel to a major city to see Cobb play. In the years before television, Cobb's appearance on a big screen in 1917 generated a lot of interest and excitement.

The year 1916 also saw Cobb build the first modern apartment building in downtown Augusta at 10th and Greene Streets. The *Augusta Herald* on

September 17, 1916, wrote about the opening of Cobb's latest business venture, saying, "The Shirley Apartments at Tenth and Greene streets are nearing completion and will be ready for opening October 1st. The Shirley is the last word in apartment house construction and elegancy and convenience marks it in every respect. There is no apartment house of its size anywhere in the South which is more elegant, and the owners of the property, the United Apartment Company, have spared neither pains nor expense in making it the most desirable possible.

"The Shirley is owned principally by Ty Cobb, the Augustan who is the most celebrated ball player the world has ever known. Ty believes in Augusta real estate and, when he saw there was not a single modern apartment house in Augusta, he decided to invest in one. There are, of course, other stockholders but Ty is the principal one. The Shirley is named for Mr. Cobb's little daughter. Mrs. Cobb was Miss Charlie Lombard of this city." [20]

In spite of being involved in all of those business ventures in 1916, as well as with his playing season, he still found time to inspire others. The *Chronicle* reported on February 6, 1916, "The boys of the Houghton School are naturally quite elated over the fact that Mr. Ty Cobb has consented to act as coach for the Houghton Baseball team in the Ne-Hi League."

Cobb, in late 1917, entered into another big business venture that was really ahead of its time: a nonalcoholic substitute for beer!

The *Chronicle* reprinted an article from the *Detroit News* that said the beer was being made by one of the largest breweries in St. Louis. Cobb was to be a sales agent for the cities of Augusta and Macon, Georgia, and the territories adjacent to each. That especially was significant because, as the article observed, each city had a large army camp that would give Cobb the opportunity to sell the nonalcoholic beer to about twenty-five thousand soldiers.

The year 1917 had started off in pretty normal fashion for Ty Cobb with his Augusta-area family, friends, and fans reading about their hometown

---

20 For a while the three-story, brick building went through several years as the run-down Shirley Hotel before being purchased by Merry Land and Investment Company, which invested $500,000 restoring it into eighteen one-bedroom and three two-bedroom apartments. It reopened as The Cobb House in November of 1984 but still has the name "Shirley" engraved in concrete above the door facing 10th Street.

hero caught up in another baseball altercation, this time in the third inning of an exhibition game in Dallas, Texas, played between the New York Giants and the Tigers. On April 1, the *Chronicle* reported that the previous day Cobb had been sliding into a base and "spiked" the left leg of Buck Herzog, causing a long gash. "Cobb and Herzog quickly came to blows," the story related. "[Shortstop Art] Fletcher came to the aid of Herzog, who was being pummeled by Cobb and soon the players of both teams joined in the fight. Police finally separated the combatants and the game proceeded after Cobb had been banished by the umpires. Clashes were frequent throughout the game and [Giants manager John] McGraw and [Tigers manager Hughie] Jennings were kept busy checking threatened renewals of hostilities.

"Cobb and Herzog again came to blows at a hotel here . . . In the encounter Herzog was struck over the eye and the skin broken. Cobb announced he would not play in any more games of the series between the Detroit club and the New York Nationals, and he decided the action of the umpires today was unfair in putting him out of the game while Herzog was permitted to continue to play."

Just a few days after Cobb and Herzog fought, U.S. President Woodrow Wilson went before Congress and asked its members to vote for a declaration of war against Germany. Congress complied on April 6, 1917. On May 18, 1917, passed the Selective Service Act authorizing the president to increase the military establishment of the United States by means of a draft. Every male living in the United States between the ages of eighteen and forty-five was required to register, including thirty-year-old Ty Cobb.

Cobb's signed draft registration card is among the Selective Service System's World War I draft registration cards, in the custody of the National Archives-Southeast Region. On the card Cobb gave his age as thirty; his name as "Tyrus R. Cobb"; home address as "2425 Williams, Augusta, Ga."; place of birth as "Narrows, Ga., U.S.A." Under the sections for present occupation, by whom employed, and where employed Cobb wrote: "Ball Player, Detroit Baseball Co., Detroit, Mich."

On January 19, 1918, the *Chronicle's* headline read, Ty Cobb Placed in Class i By Board, with a subhead reading World's Premier Ball Player To Shoulder A Gun.

According to the story, "Although Tyrus Raymond Cobb, king of the national past time, has a wife and three children, officials of the Exemption Board No. 2 have placed him in Section 1, Class 1, taking the position that his family is not dependent on him for support. Section 1 includes all registrants not included in any other division of the schedule.

"When informed last night of the action of the board, Cobb declared he is ready to shoulder a gun when the government calls him. It is probable, however, that he will not be drawn in the next draft, as his order number is 1368, a good distance down the 'at call' list."

Cobb either had second thoughts of his strong words about being ready to shoulder a gun or else was referring to a hunting rifle. Because a few days later on January 23, the newspaper reported, "Tyrus Raymond Cobb yesterday appeared before Exemption Board No. 2 and protested having been placed in first class. Investigation showed he had failed to properly fill out that section of his questionnaire covering the dependency of his wife and three children. He was reclassified, being placed in Class 2, Section A."

As thousands of American men kept dying overseas in Europe, it became increasingly difficult for Cobb not to join the fray no matter if he had a family deferment, especially in light of headlines as the one in the *Chronicle* on July 20, 1918, reading, BASEBALL PLAYERS OF DRAFT AGE MUST WORK OR FIGHT.

Secretary of War Newton Baker decided playing professional baseball was a "non-productive occupation" and baseball players and entertainers—both at that time exempt from draft—now would be subject to the draft as was most every other occupation. Baker said the scope of the draft "should be enlarged as to include other classes of persons whose professional occupation is solely that of entertaining."

On August 18, 1918, came the inevitable headline, TY COBB GOING INTO THE ARMY; QUITTING BASEBALL FOR GOOD. The *Chronicle* related Cobb had passed a physical examination—which was almost certain considering the shape he kept himself—for a commission in the gas and flame division of the U.S. Army with Cobb expressing a desire to serve in France. Cobb, according to the *Chronicle*, was quoted in a Pittsburgh, Pennsylvania, newspaper as saying he did not know anything about soldiering and his best duty occupation probably would be that of an athletic instructor.

Cobb himself was quoted as saying going into the army meant he would be leaving baseball for all time. Doomsayers were quick to share Cobb's early opinion his military service would mean the end of his illustrious baseball career. Jack Keene in his column, "Dishing Up the Sport Dope," in the *Chronicle* on September 22, 1918, wrote, "It is extremely doubtful if Cobb ever will return to the diamond. He is married and has children. He has made his pile in the game. Added to those facts is the more important one that Cobb is approaching the age at which a ball player finds it hard to keep his speed, skill and ambition. So it is a pretty good bet that the .380 mark [Cobb ended his 1918 season with] is Cobb's farewell record."

An unsigned article in the *Chronicle* on Sunday, September 29, headlined, TY COBB LEAVES AUGUSTA MONDAY TO REPORT FOR SERVICE IN ARMY, also glumly told readers, "The Georgia Peach has probably played his last game of professional baseball. He intimated this in a speech at the Polo Grounds in New York just before the season closed.

"If so, his brilliant baseball career came to a close with the adjournment of the great game until after the war is won; for it is generally conceded by all sport writers that there will be no more professional baseball till then and that the game will be on a far different status when it is resumed. And after all, what would the game be without Cobb and the other great stars who are now with the colors?"

The *Herald* reported Cobb spent the morning of September 30 saying good-bye to friends before catching the afternoon train for Washington, D.C., to report for service in the chemical warfare division. "Good-bye until I see you again," Cobb was quoted saying to many friends who, according to the *Herald*, "believe the indomitable fire and spirit that placed him at the top rung of the baseball ladder of fame will make him one of the finest of soldiers and that as Captain Cobb he will bat over .400 in his branch of the service."

Cobb apparently did not see any direct action in France, but he did have a close call during a gas chamber—chemical warfare—training exercise. The story goes that Cobb and another pro ballplayer, Christy Mathewson, were marched with other soldiers into the gas chamber. They were to put on their gas masks immediately after someone in charge gave a hand signal, moments after the chemical gas was released. But somehow many soldiers including Cobb and Mathewson missed the hand signal, and they inhaled more gas than they should have done in the training exercise. Sixteen of the men ended up stretched out on the ground needing treatment, with eight of them dying, Cobb related. When Mathewson[21] was later diagnosed with tuberculosis in both of his lungs while playing for the New York Giants, Cobb and many others believed it was a result of that fateful day in France.

Ty Cobb's time in service was incredibly brief, lasting only about two and one half months. He had left Augusta on the morning of September 30 and was back in Augusta before his thirty-second birthday. It didn't take long for the press to find him and ask what he planned to do. The headline on the *Chronicle* of December 17 told his intentions: CAPTAIN TY COBB To QUIT BASEBALL.

The article quoted the great Cobb as saying, "I'm going down to my home in Augusta, Ga., and rest up for several months. I intend to break away from baseball. I'm tired of it. I've had 15 years of it, and I want to quit while I'm still good. There is the danger that the fascination of the game has its hold on me, but I shall make every effort to tear away from it and not sign with any club again.

"When I say this, I naturally assume the release that the managers gave us last fall, with its ten days notice, is binding, and that they have no legal strings on me now. I hope so at least. I've made no plans whatever ahead of my rest. I haven't a profession because I left school at 17 to play ball."

The newspaper article added, "Cobb declared that the war had rejuvenated baseball and that it's going to boom this season as it's never done before. Cobb explained that when the armistice was signed he had just finished his training and expected to be assigned to a division which would soon see 'some real action' and declared the American Army 'has the finest personnel

---

21 Mathewson died in 1925 at the age of forty-five, and in 1936 he would be among the first batch of players voted into the National Baseball Hall of Fame along with Honus Wagner, Walter Johnson, Babe Ruth, and, of course, his former army buddy, Ty Cobb.

on earth, with everyone on his toes and wide awake every minute.'"

The *Augusta Herald*, on December 20, 1918, headlined, CAPTAIN TY COBB BACK IN AUGUSTA FROM "OVER THERE," and reiterated in the article some of the points Cobb had raised in New York City two days earlier. "I'm going to try and break away from baseball," he said to a reporter, "but I can't say the fascination of the game won't be strong enough to carry me back again—remember I said that I am going to try to quit the game."

Cobb was letting the Detroit ownership and management know if they wanted his services they had better come up with a very good deal. The bidding wars for his services began almost immediately with the *Chronicle* on Friday, December 27, 1918, reporting New York Americans (Yankees) manager Miller Huggins was visiting in Augusta, and the Americans apparently wanted to sign Cobb.

The *Chronicle* said that Cobb, Huggins, and a couple of Cobb's friends had left Augusta the previous day on a hunting trip and were expected back either Saturday night or Sunday morning. "It is recalled by Cobb's friends that the New York Americans have several times made an effort to secure Cobb," the newspaper article said. "Several years ago when Cobb and President Navin of the Detroits were seemingly so far apart on the salary question that reconciliation appeared impossible, report had it that the New York Americans made an offer of $100,000 to Detroit for Cobb.

"Cobb and Navin, however, arranged their affairs and Cobb continued with Detroit. Fifty thousand dollars is the largest purchase price ever actually paid one baseball club to another to secure the services of a single ball player; this price being paid by the Chicago Americans for Eddie Collins, then a member of the Philadelphia Athletics."

When Cobb got back into Augusta from his weekend adventure, the *Chronicle* noted he had been to Summit, Georgia, with his good Augusta friends Frank Calhoun, Jim Barrett, and Jordan Sanford. Cobb was very coy when asked if New York manager Huggins also was on that trip. "As to my having had a conference with Miller Huggins of the New York Americans, I will say that I know nothing at all of it," Cobb was quoted as saying. "I haven't seen Mr. Huggins nor heard from him, and the report that he was in

Augusta to see me was a mere rumor, so far as I know.

"As to whether I will play baseball this season, I am at present unable to answer," Cobb continued. "I am not much interested in the matter just now, and frankly am making but few plans to play.

"This I know, however, that prior to the close of the 1918 baseball season, I was handed my ten day's notice of release, as specified in the contract, which expired at the end of the playing season. The contract has been in effect for four years. Whether I go back to Detroit or whether I go with another club, I will have to sign another contract.

"Understand, however, I make no claims to be a free agent. There are rules and rules that bind a baseball contract that but few people understand, and I'm not worrying about them. I've leaving that to the Detroit club, and the National Association.

"Yes, I would consider such an offer [from another club] for under the rules of baseball no club can approach a man bound to another club without the consent of the other club or unless the man is free. Therefore should another club approach me, I should think I was free to consider their offer and that Detroit no longer had any ties to me. Should anything come of such a consideration on my part that would be contrary to the views of the Detroit club, why then the club that approached me would be liable to fine for violating the rules of the game."

A few weeks later, on March 18, 1919, the *Chronicle* told readers in a headline, TY COBB WILL SIGN CONTRACT. The story said Cobb was not going to be a holdout and expected to sign a contract "within a week or two" with the Detroit Tigers. He admitted that Hughie Jennings, Tigers manager, had come to Augusta to talk with him about his contract en route to Macon, Georgia, where the Tigers were in spring training.

Cobb said, however, he was making no arrangements to join the team in training, 125 miles from Augusta, until his contract was worked out. "I will play with Detroit this year, providing certain little details now under consideration can be arranged satisfactory to me," he said. "There are a few things I want settled, and, after that is done, I will sign but not otherwise."

Cobb signed his contract on April 8, then left Augusta to join the Tigers who were en route to Rock Hill, South Carolina, for an exhibition game against the team from Boston. Cobb told the *Chronicle* before leaving, in spite of having no spring training, he was "in excellent physical condition and fit in every way."

Apparently, he was right for in the game in Rock Hill on April 9, 1919—his first after his military service—Cobb "drove out a home run on his first appearance at bat in the first inning." Boston nevertheless won the game, 5–3.

Cobb was back in a Tigers uniform on April 25, when the Tigers began the American League season in Detroit with a 4–2 victory over Cleveland. The account in the *Chronicle* on April 26 would note, "Four hits in third inning, one of them a double by Cobb, coupled with [Stan] Coveleskie's error, gave Detroit a lead the visitors were unable to overcome."

The world of baseball was about to learn exactly the stuff from which legends are made.

He finished the 1919 season with a batting average of .384. Cobb had played in 124 games, batting 497 times, making 191 hits, including 1 home run, that resulted in 92 runs batted in. He also stole 28 bases.

And the next year on his thirty-fourth birthday, Cobb would sign another contract with Tigers owner Navin making Cobb both manager and player and baseball's highest-paid star at a salary of $30,000 per year.

# Becoming Player-Manager
## of the Tigers                                                    10

The entry for Ty Cobb in the Augusta city directory in 1921 read: "COBB, TYRUS R (Charlie M), Pres Ty Cobb Tire Co., h 2425 Williams, Tel 6667."

Going into his own tire business in Augusta in 1919 right after leaving the service at the end of World War I was a natural transition for Cobb, who long had been interested in automobiles and who must have been in car heaven in Detroit. He frequently spent his off-seasons going to automobile races in Augusta and Savannah, Georgia, and elsewhere, where he often was the "official starter."

So it was not very surprising when Cobb joined with Bill Sanford, a former grammar school principal, in the tire business, located at 662 Broad Street on the corner of what is now Broad and Seventh Streets.

Cobb and Sanford, long-time hunting buddies, also included in their venture another hunting pal, Frank Bussey. The advertisements in October and early November of 1919 for the Ty Cobb-Bill Sanford Tire Company offered Pennsylvania Vacuum Cup as well as Goodyear tires. Printed in the advertisements were the names of Cobb, Bussey, and Sanford, along with the store's phone number, 1357, and its slogan, "Square Deal and Service First."

But something serious may have happened between the hunting buddies. In April of 1920 Cobb legally changed the name of the tire business from Ty Cobb-Bill Sanford Tire Company to just Ty Cobb Tire Company.

And about that same time, Cobb sold the property in which the company was housed to the L. A. Russell Piano Company for $50,000. He reportedly had paid $45,000 for the property and made improvements to it, with a marble front (that still can be seen today) and a two-story brick addition on Seventh Street.[22] The tire store remained open at the site into 1921, with the business selling Green Flag motor oil and bicycle tires as well as the Pennsylvania Vacuum Cup and Diamond tires, but the store went bankrupt in January of 1922.

It's a mystery what exactly happened to the store and why it did go bankrupt, because surely Cobb with his growing wealth and influence could have saved the company from bankruptcy if he had chosen to do so. The saga of the Ty Cobb Tire Company marked one of the few true failures of Cobb's off-the-field business endeavors. But even if the tire store business didn't work out as he expected, Cobb had a talent called baseball that he could fall back upon.

Just a few months before Cobb ended his 1920 season, he suffered a serious injury that threatened to put him out of commission for the rest of the season. The *Chronicle* on June 25, 1920, headlined a story, TY COBB DENIES REPORT THAT HE IS OUT OF GAME, with the article saying, two weeks earlier playing Chicago, Cobb had torn three ligaments of his right knee sliding into base. The week after his injury he came home to Augusta to recuperate.

On June 27, the *Chronicle* reported Cobb had umpired a game between two North Augusta and Augusta amateur teams with the North Augusta team winning 12–4. "The game was practically without features, except for entire lack of argument with Umps, who had apparently witnessed a few other games of the national past time," the *Chronicle* reported tongue in

---

22 The building many years later would be used by WGAC radio station and also by a law firm that had as its partner Carl E. Sanders, the only native Augustan in the twentieth century to become governor of Georgia.

cheek. "We will have to hand it to him, our friend Tyrus Raymond is some umpire and would recommend that Mr. Walsh sign him up."

On July 5, at Bowles Race Track in Richmond County, Cobb was the judge of horse races. The advertisement for the races noted, "Some of the best horses in this section and adjoining towns will enter. Special arrangements will be made for ladies. Races will begin promptly at 3 o'clock. Trucks will carry passengers from 9th and Gwinnett [now Laney-Walker Boulevard] to Race Track, 12:30 and 1:30 o'clock. Admission to races, 50 cents. A big barbecue dinner will be served all day, so come on out and show your sporting blood."

After the rest and relaxation in Augusta, in typical Cobb fashion he was back in the game within weeks. The *Augusta Herald* reported on July 6, 1920, "Ty Cobb, the world's greatest baseball player leaves his home in this city today to join the Tigers in New York.

"As is known, Cobb was injured about a month ago while his team was playing at Chicago. In a run-in in the garden, Cobb tore three ligaments in his knee. The injury was very painful and there were some who said that Cobb would not be able to return to the Bengal fold this season, but the Georgian recovered rapidly and is now in such shape that he will be able to resume play in a very few days."

Cobb not only got back into condition as a player and finished his 1920 season with a batting average of .334, but he also was in condition to take on an even greater role in his baseball career by becoming player-manager of the Tigers.

"I very much should have preferred to lay aside all ambitions in the managerial line until such time as I felt myself slipping," Cobb said, noting he did not seek the position but accepted it because Navin insisted the team needed him as a leader. "I know I have several years of good baseball ahead of me," Cobb continued. "Now that I have decided to take the plunge, I intend to be the best manager. I will fight and fight hard to make myself as successful a leader as I have been a player. In the meantime I do not intend to allow any chance managerial burdens to detract from my play."

Anyone knowing Cobb's fierce determination on the diamond would not have expected otherwise.

Oddly enough, one of the first persons in the entire world to know Cobb had become the Tigers player-manager was none other than W. V. "Bill" Woodward, manager of the Ty Cobb Tire Company. Sportswriter Earl Bell, a friend of Cobb's, wrote in the *Augusta Herald* on Sunday, December 19, 1920, "Augusta 'broke' this piece of important news late Saturday afternoon [in the *Herald*] before it became known in northern cities. Immediately after affixing his John Hancock to the contract, Cobb wired the news to W. V. Woodward, manager of the Ty Cobb Tire Company, and Bill, with Cobb's consent, promptly notified the Augusta newspaper. The story was later put on the wires from New York."

Bell said it wasn't disclosed in the initial news but Cobb's reported salary as player-manager would be $30,000. That was borne out by the *Chronicle* on December 26, when it published a photo of Navin and Cobb at the contract signing and confirmed the salary figure.

Cobb was back home in late 1920 and early 1921, but he left Augusta on Saturday, January 29, 1921, bound for Detroit and a banquet to be held in his honor on Tuesday night, February 1. The *Chronicle* wrote about that banquet a week later on February 8 in an editorial entitled, REMARKABLE TRIBUTE TO TY COBB. The newspaper told its readers and Cobb's local friends and fans just how grand the banquet turned out to be.

"That night nearly a thousand—more than nine hundred—citizens entertained him at a banquet, at which there were present some of the most prominent men in America known to baseball and to which were sent messages of greeting from others equally as prominent in baseball.

"The tribute to Cobb was a remarkable one. It was the assurance of the full support of the people of Detroit to him as manager of the club. More than that, it was an attest of the splendid regard in which Cobb is held, personally and as a ball player, by Detroit, and throughout the country.

"It is accomplishing a great deal to attend the highest place in one's calling. Cobb is the world's greatest baseball player. He has played on no other big league club than Detroit's. That the people of that city, at this time, so outspokenly endorse him is the highest praise that could be given him. If good wishes and good will can count—the good wishes and good will not only of Augusta and Detroit but of friends and admirers throughout the country—Cobb as baseball manager will be as successful as Cobb as baseball player."

In January of 1922, Cobb was announcing that final arrangements had been made with James U. Jackson, founder of the town of North Augusta, South Carolina, and his brother, George, to house the Tigers during their 1922 spring training in the Jacksons' two white-columned, Southern-style mansions in North Augusta.[23]

"Cobb will have a secretary come to Augusta ahead of the team and make all arrangements necessary such as hiring cooks, waiters and other employees," the *Chronicle* said on January 11, 1922. "The houses will accommodate about 20 men each and they will eat and sleep there. A manager of quarters will be appointed by Cobb and will take charge of running the houses for the players."

The Tigers got settled in Augusta before heading to Atlanta for exhibition games. "Manager Ty Cobb will take 15 men on the trip to Atlanta for the two games with Georgia Tech Thursday and Friday, it was learned last night. The Tiger team will leave here tonight," the *Chronicle* reported on Wednesday, March 15.

"It is very probable that only recruit pitchers will be used in the game with the collegians and the manager [Cobb] will thereby have the opportunity of seeing them in action in a real game," the newspaper added. "It is a principle of the Detroit manager that his pitchers only use fast ones and no curve balls in the games with college teams, it is learned. This is done in order that he might see his fielders in action."

On Saturday, March 18, 1922, Augusta baseball fans got an incredible treat in getting to see Cobb's major-league Tigers play native Augustan George Stallings's minor-league Rochester Tribe at Warren Park with Cobb playing in the game. "For the first time in three years, Augusta fans will have the opportunity of seeing Ty Cobb in action at Warren Park," the *Chronicle* had said earlier. "The Detroit Tigers and the Rochester team will

---

23 George Jackson's mansion built in 1895 and now known as Lookaway Hall, located at the intersection of Georgia and Carolina Avenues, and James Jackon's similar mansion, Rosemary Hall, built in 1902, located on Carolina Avenue across from Lookaway Hall, are now popular bed-and-breakfast homes where many wedding receptions are held.

meet there Saturday afternoon at 3 o'clock. A young manager will test his warriors against the ability of a seasoned pilot with a lower class team. Cobb against Stallings—both of them Augustans, the former by adoption and the latter by birth."

Stallings actually had been Cobb's own personal choice to become the manager of the 1921 Detroit team, according to *Augusta Herald* sportswriter Earl Bell, who had quoted Cobb as saying, "I have recommended George Stallings, and I hope he will be given this job. I know no man who could do more to convert a losing team into a winner. In my opinion, the Detroit Club needs a manager like Stallings."

As if Augusta fans weren't impressed enough with the legendary Cobb and Stallings bringing their teams to town to do battle, there was an extra treat a few days before the game with a visit by the current baseball commissioner himself, Judge Kenesaw Mountain Landis, who arrived March 13, for a one-day visit as the guest of Cobb. Augusta was the first stop for Landis's tour of 1922 spring training camps.

Landis had been elected baseball's first commissioner on November 12, 1920. He was born in Millville, Ohio, but his first name came from Kennesaw Mountain in Georgia near Atlanta, where his father, Abraham Landis, was seriously wounded during the Civil War.

On March 14, the *Chronicle* would report of Landis's visit, "At the Cobb home on Williams Street, The Hill, he received newspapermen, meeting them in a most cordial manner, but speaking very little on the subject of baseball.

"At the very beginning of the interview he apologized by saying, 'I trust you will pardon me for I am very poor copy tonight.'

"The baseball arbiter stated that he was making the tour of the training camps in order to see the managers and men and to become acquainted with them. 'As there are rookies in baseball and everything else,' he said, 'so am I a rookie in my new business. I want to know the players and therefore I am visiting the training camps.'"

The *Chronicle* additionally noted, "It was a striking little gathering at Cobb's home. There were two of the greatest men in baseball, one a commissioner and the other a manager and player. Engaged in far different activities, the two of them, nevertheless, working toward the same goal—clean sportsmanlike baseball for the millions of fans in the United States."

Cobb's second season in his dual role of player-manager also was his third and last season hitting more than .400. He had played in 137 games with 526 at bats resulting in 211 hits and 99 runs including 4 home runs.

His continued success and growing fame continued to attract the attention of America's leading citizens with U.S. president Warren G. Harding and his wife, Florence, heading out to Warren Park on the Tuesday afternoon of April 3, 1923, to see Cobb play. [24]

Like Taft, Harding loved golf, and during his 1923 visit to Augusta he played not only at the Augusta Country Club not far from Cobb's home but also at the Palmetto course in nearby Aiken, South Carolina. He also watched a polo match at Whitney Field in Aiken during his excursion there.

The *Chronicle* on April 4 reported, "President Harding put one over on the most of the other baseball fans of the country yesterday by slipping out to Warren Park here to see an exhibition game between the Detroit Americans and the Toronto [Canada] club of the International League.

"The chief executive was accompanied by Mrs. Harding who seemed to enjoy the game as much as her husband who is quite a baseball fan and used to own stock in a club at Marion, Ohio. They went to the game accompanied by half a dozen other members of their party as the guest of former Judge Landis, high commissioner of baseball.

"Arriving at the park just a few minutes before the game time, the President took a seat on a lower row of the grandstand, asked for a score card, listed the line-up and got set for the game. Before the game started, Ty Cobb, an Augusta product and manager of the Detroit club, and Dan Howley, manager of the Toronto club, came into the stand and shook hands with the President and Mrs. Harding; they having met and become friends before Mr. Harding became President or Mr. Cobb became a club manager.

---

24 Harding is one of the most underrated presidents in regard to his love of baseball, but, in fact, he even owned a minor-league team in Marion, Ohio, where he once was editor and publisher of the *Marion Star* and where he now is entombed. He had Babe Ruth as a guest in the White House at least seven times during his brief administration, and he once was said to have remarked about baseball, "I never saw a game without taking sides and never want to see one. There is the soul of the game."

"During the innings, it looked as though the President would be cheated out of seeing a full game by an April shower, but the rain stopped in time to save the game," the account said. "The President kept score as carefully as any of the fans, and he and Mrs. Harding joined in the cheering when Dell Pratt, the Detroit second baseman, knocked a home run over the left field fence in the fourth inning. The game resulted in a 9 to 2 victory for Detroit."

Cobb got two hits in that game and scored a run. The next month on May 25, Cobb would score his 1,741st run to pass another legend, Pittsburgh Pirate Honus Wagner.

On June 30, 1923, Charlie Cobb's father, Roswell Oliver Lombard, died about 6:00 p.m. that Saturday in the old University Hospital. He was sixty-three and was described at his death as "one of Augusta's wealthiest and most prominent citizens."

The *Chronicle* noted, "His home is nine miles from the city on the Dean's Bridge Road. His farm land holdings comprise thousands of acres of the finest stretch in the county. His home place is beautifully located and the improvements are most attractive. Mr. Lombard owned much desirable city property. The Modjeska Theater, built directly after the 1916 fire, was put up by him and belonged to him. He owned other valuable city real estate.

"Mr. Lombard led the life of a well-to-do farmer and businessman, respected by his neighbors and enjoying the high regard of all who knew him. He did not care for public life, though at one time he was prevailed to accept a county commissionership. He served for a long time on that board, giving valuable service to the county; his extended experience and his high business ability well equipping him for membership on the commission.

"Mr. Lombard is survived by his wife, Mrs. Nancy Jones Lombard; two sons, Mr. Alfred Oliver Lombard and Mr. Roswell Harmond Lombard; and one daughter, Mrs. Tyrus R. Cobb. There are ten grandchildren. Mr. Lombard was the brother of George R. Lombard."

Roswell Lombard was buried in Magnolia Cemetery near his daughter, Frances, who had died four years earlier on January 16, 1919.

Ty Cobb and his Tigers in Augusta in March of 1924 for spring training were the guests of the Kiwanis Club of Augusta at a barbecue at Carmichael's, the same place where Commissioner Landis had been a guest.

One interesting article written in 1924 was by sportswriter Grantland Rice, who not only covered Cobb's baseball exploits from the very first but also golfed with him frequently. The subject of Rice's article was how a player deals with a batting slump that often haunts major- and minor-league players. "It's a queer thing," said Cobb, "how a player without knowing it can change his position at bat; just enough perhaps to throw him off. He may shift his feet and not know that he has made any shift. When I get going badly, I ask some one in whose judgment I have confidence to see what I am doing wrong. I find one help is to face the pitcher a little more squarely and to raise my right elbow to hit more on a line, rather than up or down.

"The most important part of a slump is to watch the mental side. After one or two hitless games, it is hard to keep from worrying and from over-trying. The same thing happens in golf when you're missing a few shots in a row. When a ballplayer is in a batting slump he is inclined to become over-anxious and over-eager, to get his body in too quickly and to hit too quickly. There can't be any rhythm or timing to your swing when there's worry or an upset in your brain.

"I still claim that the golf swing and the baseball swing are quite different. In golf, the ball sits there until you hit it and the stroke is down—not on a line. In baseball, you are hitting at a moving object. Co-ordination must be far quicker. A few feet from the plate, you see the ball begin to curve. In less than a fifth of a second, the eye telegraphs the news to the brain and the brain shoots its message onto the muscles. Instinct must do the rest and start the bat where you figure the curve will break. But you often have the change the course of your swing after it has started.

"I'm certain of one thing—and that is that baseball or tennis or almost any other game is no help to golf. You can't mix up another game with golf and play good golf."

Years later in 1944, professional golfer Byron Nelson—winner of the 1937 and 1942 Masters Tournaments at the Augusta National course in Augusta—would tell of a visit to Cobb's home when Cobb only wanted to talk about golf. He recalled: "Cobb was wondering how you could shake off a slump in your golf game. I asked him how he shook off a batting slump.

He said he would go out to the field and practice bunting, then swing easily at the ball, gradually working up to a full swing.

"I told him that when I was off on my golf game I'd do practically the same thing. That is, I'd start working with the short clubs and gradually work up to the long woods.

"Cobb apparently hadn't thought of using the same system he used in baseball in correcting a golf slump [and said] 'By George, I'll try that.'"

The late Augusta city councilman I. E. "Ike" Washington recalled the friendship between Grantland Rice and Cobb: "When I was in high school, I used to caddy at the Augusta Country Club whenever I could because my family needed the money. Once I caddied for Grantland Rice, the great sportswriter. Ty Cobb was his host.

"All the way around the course, the other caddies told me, 'You're going to get a GOOD tip because you're caddying for Mr. Rice.' But when we got in after eighteen holes, Mr. Rice reached for his wallet, and Ty Cobb said, 'No, no, Grant. You're in my hometown. I'll take care of it,' and Ty Cobb handed me just a brand new dollar."

Cobb's love of doing fun things in his hometown even extended in early 1925 to horseshoes as the *Chronicle* noted in a story published on January 22. The article reported that more than 200 delegates to the National Furniture Warehousemen's fifth semiannual meeting "yesterday took part in a golf tournament and putting contest on the Country Club links, while Ty Cobb umpired a horseshoe throwing contest on the club green. Tomorrow will be a big day for the visitors for in the afternoon the ladies will attend a fashion show at the J. B. White department store while the men will participate in a coon [raccoon] and possom hunt followed by a weiner roast tomorrow night."

Imagine the faces on those out-of-town delegates when the greatest ballplayer in the world showed up to umpire a horseshoe-pitching contest!

On March, 11, 1925, Cobb joined "the entire Detroit baseball team" in the Imperial Theater in downtown Augusta as the invited guests of Robert B. Mantell, the famous American Shakespeare tragedian, who with a touring company was performing selections from *The Merchant of Venice*, *As You Like It*, and *Macbeth*.

When Cobb became manager of the Tigers in addition to being a player, he told reporters he did not intend to let any managerial burdens detract from his play. And, Lord, was he right as he proved in his best-ever game on May 5, 1925, playing against the St. Louis Browns in St. Louis. He hit 3 home runs, 1 double, and 2 singles. The *Chronicle* headline the next day read: TY COBB TIES RECORD WITH THREE HOMERS IN ONE GAME; GETS SIX OUT OF SIX TRIES.

"Tying the modern major league record the veteran Ty Cobb, playing manager of the Detroit Tigers, pulled out three home runs in today's game with the St. Louis Browns. They were off Pitchers [Joe] Bush, [Elam] Vangilder and [Milt] Gaston," the *Chronicle* related.

"Cobb, who led the American league in batting for nine consecutive years, is playing his 21st season in big league baseball. He has a record of holding American batting honors from 1907 to 1915 when Tris Speaker took the lead.

"Swinging a champion's bat in 1917, Cobb again held the lead until George Sisler, manager of the St. Louis Browns, came into prominence with the highest average in 1920.

"Cobb, in smashing out six hits [in St. Louis], collected a total of 16 bases, a new world's record for modern major league baseball. His three homers tied the record for this specialty in modern major league baseball and he also collected a double and two singles.

"The previous record for modern baseball was held by Eddie [Edward Patrick "Patsy"] Gharrity, Washington catcher, who ran his total of bases for one game to 13 in June 1919.

"The old record made before the advent of the American league was held jointly by Bobby Lowe of the Boston Nationals, who, in 1894, collected four homers and a single, and Ed Delahanty of the Philadelphia Nationals, duplicated the stunt in 1896. Each of these players had a total of 17 bases.

"The only other major league players who have made three home runs in a single game in the 20th century [up until that time early in the twentieth century] are George Kelly of the Giants, Ken Williams of the Browns, Cy Williams of the Phillies and Walter Henline of the Phillies."

## PHIL COCKRELL

Unlike Cobb, who received almost weekly coverage in the Augusta newspapers, Augusta native Phil Cockrell was rarely mentioned even in death. Overcoming obstacles is the stuff of which athletic legends and other good folks are made, and that too was the case of Cockrell, who would create baseball history as a player and umpire in the Negro Leagues.

Phillip Williams Cockrell was born in Augusta in 1898, just twelve years after Cobb was born in Georgia, and Cockrell's playing career took place from 1917 to 1934, so he surely was aware of Cobb and surely came close to crossing Cobb's path several times both in the cities where each played ball and surely back home in Augusta where Cockrell visited relatives.

Cockrell would play for the Havana Red Sox in Cuba, New York Lincoln Giants, Hilldale Daisies, Atlantic City Bacharach Giants, and the Philadelphia Stars. He pitched for Hilldale in two Negro League World Series games in 1924 and 1925. He won the sixth and conclusive game of the 1925 World Series giving the title to Hilldale. He even replaced the famous Oscar Charleston, a main character in the Lee Blessing play *Cobb*, as manager of the Hilldale team in 1929.

In its Sunday edition on September 20, 1925, in a regular feature called "Notes Among The Colored People," the *Chronicle* ran a brief notice saying, "Have you ever heard of Phil Cockrell? Well he is an Augusta colored professional baseball player who hurls at will a no-hit-no-run game. His team plays one or two of the big league teams every year. Listen out for Cockrell in the post-League series about the first week in October, between the all-star colored team and New York Yankees at the Yankee Stadium, which has a seating capacity of 75,000. Out in the East Cockrell is good advertising for Augusta."

Cockrell also made it to the main sports page of the *Chronicle* on March 18, 1926, with a small story headlined simply, FAMOUS NEGRO PITCHER. The article by J. C. Mardexborough said, "Phil Cockrell, the no-hit, no-run pitcher for Hilldale, the champion colored baseball pitcher of this country, arrived here last night from Philadelphia. He is known the country over as one of the brightest lights in the baseball firmament today.

"He was born in this city and began his baseball career with the famous 'Pop' Watkins and like, the old master has written his name among the baseball fame most especially as a 'no hit, no run pitcher' as he is known in the East. Hilldale, his team, has met some of the best teams in the East.

"For several years Hilldale has met Connie Mack's team except last year. However they did play the Jersey City Internationals and won the best two out of three.

"Phil Cockrell is a product of Paine College and will help to work out the team while he is in the city. He is one of the highest paid colored baseball players in the game and likewise knows the game from 'A to Z.'

"Those who like the game should take the opportunity to see Cockrell work Paine out while here."

After quitting as a professional player in 1935, Cockrell became a Negro National League umpire and worked in that capacity through the 1946 season. He met an untimely end when he walked out of a bar in Philadelphia on March 31, 1951, and was shot to death by an angry man who mistakenly thought Cockrell was fooling around with the man's wife.

Not finished quite yet, Cobb went back up against the St. Louis Browns in St. Louis the next day, May 6, and got two more home runs to bring his total to five home runs in two days of major-league play. The *Chronicle* headline read, COBB GETS TWO MORE AND ANOTHER RECORD.

"Five home runs in two consecutive games constitute a new record for modern major league baseball," the *Chronicle* readers were told. "A. C. Anson of Chicago got five home runs in two consecutive games in 1884. The modern record of four was held by Babe Ruth of the Yankees, Ken Williams of the Browns and Charles Walker of the Athletics."

As he turned thirty-nine at the close of 1925, in its edition of December 18, the *Chronicle* printed a drawing of Cobb by syndicated cartoonist Feg Murray with text that noted that Cobb has "played in 2,725 games, been at bat 10,353 times, scored 2,038 runs, made 3,823 hits, stolen 856 bases" and whose batting average for twenty-one seasons was .369.

"Ty That!" Murray wrote with his drawing.

Considering that enormous career achievement at the age of thirty-nine, it still would be a blow to baseball fans the world over when, the next year, Tyrus Raymond Cobb announced he was quitting baseball forever.

# QUITTING THE GAME
# AND FACING A SCANDAL          11

THE SPRING OF 1926 FOUND Ty Cobb not only bringing the Detroit Tigers back to Augusta for spring training for the fourth—and what would be the last—consecutive year but also putting on an Augusta team uniform for the first time since leaving the old Tourists team in 1905.

TY COBB TO PLAY CENTERFIELD FOR AUGUSTA SATURDAY read the headline of the *Herald* of March 31, 1926. The story said it had been a long time since Cobb "held down the middle sector of Warren Park." Then it added, "Time moves in cycles, they say, and on Saturday, Ty, now recognized as the greatest player the game has produced, will again don the toggery of his home town.

"The manager of the Detroit Tigers Tuesday night requested that he be permitted to play centerfield for the Augusta Tygers [now called so in honor of you know who] at their exhibition game with his own Bengals. Needless to say the request was granted.

"And Ty will also lend [Augusta] Manager 'Gabby' Street a few of his pitchers to make the match the more interesting."

In the rematch of the March 28, 1905, Augusta-Detroit matchup, when Cobb first took center field against the Tigers, the score was not even close with Detroit topping Augusta, 12–3. The headline, however, noted positively, COBB, PLAYING CENTERFIELD FOR LOCALS, GETS DOUBLE AND SINGLE IN FOUR TRIES.

The recap of the game on April 4, 1926, in the *Augusta Herald* read: "The slugging Detroit Tigers, led by Heinie Manush with two home runs and two singles, severely spanked the Augusta Tygers here Saturday afternoon, 12 to 3, in the first and only exhibition game of the season between these two outfits. Ty Cobb played in centerfield for the Augusta club and he permitted the locals to use two of his pitchers. Ty got a double and a single for his home town."

It was noted the Detroit team would leave Augusta that night and play several exhibition games on their way back to Michigan. "The Tigers had splendid training weather while here," the *Herald* noted, "being able to practice here every day, which was better than the record of any other big league training camp.

"Detroit's training here this spring marked the fourth consecutive year that the team has been Augusta's guests, and Ty Cobb stated yesterday that he hoped to bring the Bengals back next season."

The writer of the unsigned article—more than likely Cobb's good friend Earl Bell—closed with the personal note, "Good luck, Ty." And by the end of 1926, Cobb certainly would need all the luck he could get and then some as he would be drawn into one of baseball's ugliest scandals, with Cobb himself accused of cheating to throw a game.

In late October 1926, Ty Cobb went on a hunting trip in Canada with Cleveland player and manager Tris Speaker. It is not known exactly what they talked about on that trip, but Cobb must have shared some concerns about his future in baseball with Speaker, especially in light of the Tigers again failing to win a pennant and with stadium attendance down.

On the morning of November 4, 1926, Augustans awoke to a huge headline stretching totally across the top of the *Chronicle's* front page shouting in big, bold, black letters: TY COBB QUITS BASEBALL.

Some readers may have been skeptical when remembering that just seven years earlier in February of 1919, Cobb, after being discharged from the army, also talked about quitting baseball. But this time, it was clear that Cobb wasn't playing a game or being coy to get a better contract with the Tigers. This time he was serious.

Cobb told a reporter for the Associated Press in Atlanta at a stopover on his way back to Augusta that he had been obsessed with trying to win a pennant for the Detroit fans and had worked hard for six years as manager to develop his men into a World Series winning team. "But I saw that it would be several years under existing conditions before I could turn out a winner," he added. "I wanted to quit while I was still among the best, so I just got out."

He talked about a big birthday coming up the next month but said that really didn't have anything to do with his decision. "You know I am going to be 40 years old December 18," he remarked. "I am about as good as I ever was, but the time has come for me to quit taking chances, and that means that it is time for me to get out. I don't want to be one of those men who fade or have to be pushed out."

Cobb didn't have any immediate plans other than to spend some time hunting and be with his family. "Of course I can still hit 'em," he added proudly. "I finished this season up in the 340's which you know is not so bad. It's just this: I am tired. . . . You know I have not had much time with my family. I want to settle down and live with my own folks for awhile. That's another good reason for my getting out as manager."

Thomas J. Hamilton, who now had become editor of the *Augusta Chronicle*, believing it was the end of an era, wrote a column saying, "Baseball has lost its most brilliant and most spectacular performer, if Ty Cobb has really decided to give up the great national pastime upon which he shed luster for more than 20 years and for which he did as much or more than anyone else to elevate that great dignity and popularity which professional baseball enjoys today."

Hamilton recalled how his own career as a journalist was intertwined with Cobb's rise in baseball. "I first knew him as a cub reporter in 1906, but it was two years later as sports editor of the *Chronicle* that a real friendship resulted which has continued uninterrupted through the years," Hamilton said.

He especially recalled seventeen years earlier being one of the few nonfamily invited guests when Ty and Charlie married. "I drove nine miles in the country using a horse and buggy to attend the ceremony," he wrote. "I had queried papers all over the country before leaving for the wedding, and when I returned found a huge stack of telegrams which kept me busy for hours answering them; every paper in the country wanted the story on the wedding of baseball's scintillating performer who was burning the big leagues in a style never seen before."

Hamilton concluded, "I have known him as a baseball player and have had associations with him in a business way [Cobb being a stockholder in the *Chronicle*], and have known him intimately in a personal way for many years, and I state without hesitation that I have never known a cleaner or squarer chap."

On November 3, Cobb was met at the Atlanta train station on his way home by his wife, and they stayed overnight—most likely visiting his mother and sister in Atlanta—before heading on to Augusta, arriving about 6:30 p.m., November 4.

He reiterated to reporters who met him in Augusta he just wanted to spend some time home with his family and friends. "I'm back home to stay," he said. "Augusta is my home and I have so many old friends here whom I want to see more of; to mingle with because I couldn't see much of them while playing baseball. There's something else, too. There are certain phases of life which one misses while playing baseball and managing a big league team."

In late November and early December of 1926, Cobb started showing signs of just being another average citizen in Augusta. On November 11, there was a photo of him on the front page of the *Chronicle* being pinned by a Red Cross nurse and handing the nurse one dollar for a year's membership in the American Red Cross. And on December 12, there was brief notice saying Cobb had gone to bed when reporters called on him at home to find out if a wild rumor that he was giving up living in Augusta and moving his family to France was true! Mrs. Cobb was awake and told the reporters there was no truth to the rumor but that the family was planning a vacation trip to Europe the following May when Cobb normally would be in spring training with the Tigers.

All seemed quiet on the home front as Cobb celebrated his fortieth birthday, as Christmas of 1926 rapidly approached, but then on Tuesday afternoon, December 21, the headline in the *Augusta Herald* shouted in huge, black letters, COBB AND SPEAKER MENTIONED IN NEWEST BASEBALL SCANDAL.

*Ty Cobb poses with his family in his WWI Army uniform.*

Elna Lombard Collection, Courtesy of Margaret Holley

*The ballpark in Augusta, Georgia, where Ty Cobb made his professional debut was called Warren Park.*

## WELL! WELL! WELL!

Well! Well! Well! But, anyhow, the opening game does not win the pennant. The Boston World Beaters lost their first game this season.

• • •

Cobb's two-bagger in the eighth inning started the ball rolling and almost won the game. His home run was a peacherina. He is going to make a good man.

• • •

Everybody fans at the game yesterday. Everything cheering like mad until the last man was out.

• • •

Engel, besides being a good pitcher, is also a good batter. He slammed out the first home run of the season.

• • •

Fred Hays has gone to Anniston, Ala., where he will accept a position on that team.

• • •

## FIRST BALL GAME GRAND CONTEST

TWO THOUSAND ENTHUSIASTIC ROOTERS WITNESS SKYSCRAP-ERS DEFEAT TOURISTS.

## MAGNIFICENT PLAY.

Cheering Thousands Witness Most Exciting Game on Augusta Diamond Since the Days of Stallings. Smart, Clean-Cut Article of Baseball.

*Ty Cobb's career was eagerly anticipated by the sports staff at the* Augusta Chronicle. *He would provide them column inches for years to come.*

*Cobb's stance at the plate was unmistakable even in his earliest days.*

The Augusta Chronicle

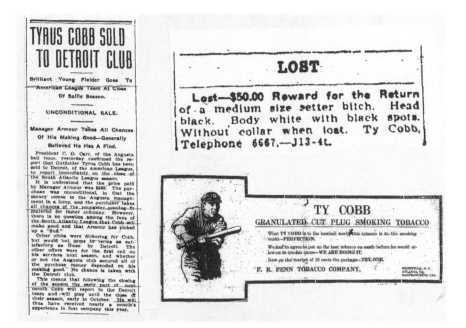

*An early contract holdout, when Cobb was "sold" to the Detroit Tigers, he argued long and hard for a better deal for himself.*

The Augusta Chronicle

*This 1908 photo of the Augusta Tourists reflects the absence of their star player, sold to the Detroit Tigers.*

Augusta Museum of History

*"The Oaks" was the home of Charlie Lombard Cobb's parents. It was here that Ty and Charlie Cobb were married in a very small, private ceremony.*
Elna Lombard Collection, Courtesy of Margaret Holley

*Ty Cobb loved playing baseball, even off-season. He got this team together in 1913 comprising players from Royston, Augusta, and the Detroit Tigers to play an exhibition game against the University of Georgia's baseball team.*
Augusta Museum of History

*Ty Cobb in his Detroit Tigers uniform, ca. 1911.*
Library of Congress

*Cobb slides into third base. His fearlessness at stealing bases is reflected in his record fifty-four times
stealing home over his career.*
Augusta Museum of History

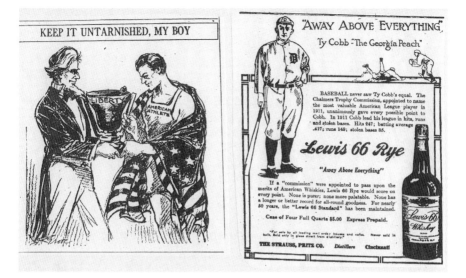

Cobb was one of the earliest professional sports figures to lend his name and image to advertising products. The cartoon on the left was in tribute to athletes enlisting for World War I.
The Augusta Chronicle

Advertising for Piedmont cigarettes appeared on the reverse side of this early Ty Cobb baseball card.
From the author's collection

Cobb's name was linked with the game's greatest players early in his career. He is pictured here with Honus Wagner, who objected to the use of tobacco advertising on his baseball cards, ca. 1909.
Library of Congress

*Cobb was a lifelong friend and admirer of the great Christy Mathewson, pictured here at the 1911 World Series. Both were in the first group of players inducted into the Baseball Hall of Fame.*

*Cobb ready to take the field in Detroit ca. 1913.*

*Cobb and "Shoeless" Joe Jackson ca. 1913, before controversy marred both of their careers.*

Library of Congress

*Cobb in his
Tigers uniform
ca. 1915.*
Library of Congress

*Cobb baseball card from
1912, issued by Honest
Long Cut and Miners
Extra brands of tobacco.*
Library of Congress

The Cobb house on Williams Street in Augusta, Georgia, where Ty and Charlie Cobb raised five children.

Don Rhodes

Charlie Cobb holds a baby at a shower she gave for her sister-in-law, Anne Lombard, at the Cobb home on Williams Street in Augusta, Georgia.

Elna Lombard Collection, Courtesy of Margaret Holley

Ty Cobb, center fielder and star of the Detroit Tigers, is seen with his family at his home in Augusta April 11, 1923. Beside Ty and his wife Charlie are the children, from left to right: Shirley, age 11, Tyrus, Jr., age 13, Baby Jimmy, Beverly, 3, and Herschel, 6.

AP Photo

When home in Augusta,
Cobb participated in many
community events. He played
the starring role in a play called
The College Widow. *Future
president of the United States,
Woodrow Wilson, was in the
audience.*
The Augusta Chronicle

*Ty Cobb and the 1923
Summerville School
Ne-Hi baseball team in
Augusta, Georgia.*
Augusta Museum of History

*The 1925 Detroit "Tygers" pose during spring training.*
The Augusta Chronicle

*When Cobb finally retired in 1926, it was front-page news in the Augusta Chronicle.*
The Augusta Chronicle

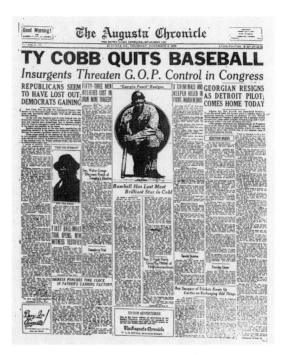

Cobb was great friends with Tris Speaker throughout their careers in baseball. Afterward, they maintained their relationship, and they are shown here on a hunting trip.
Vanishing Georgia, Georgia Division of Archives and History, Office of Secretary of State

*Cobb surrounded by children at the groundbreaking for the Cobb
Memorial Hospital in Royston, Georgia.*
Vanishing Georgia, Georgia Division of Archives and History, Office of Secretary of State

*Three of those gathered for the dedication of the
Cobb Memorial Hospital in Royston, Georgia.
From left to right: Dr. Stuart Brown, Gus Skelton
(childhood friend of Ty Cobb) and Ty Cobb.*
Vanishing Georgia, Georgia Division of Archives and History,
Office of Secretary of State

*Ty's Detroit uniform in Ty Cobb Museum
in Royston, Georgia, on loan from his
granddaughter, Peggy Cobb Schug.*
Don Rhodes

*From left: George Sisler, Babe Ruth, and Ty Cobb at the 1924 World Series.*
Library of Congress

To this day, there is controversy over who was the *"greatest ballplayer of all time"* and Cobb
and Ruth are still the top contenders.
The Augusta Chronicle

*The late Pope Welborn, owner of a service station in Cornelia, Georgia, was Cobb's running buddy in his final years. He holds a Cobb-autographed ball in front of the small, brick apartment building in Cornelia, Georgia, where Cobb lived in his later years.*
Don Rhodes

*The third and final time Ty Cobb was honored by Augustans: this time at Jennings Stadium at Allen Park on August 29, 1957, for Ty Cobb Day, four years before he died.*
The Augusta Chronicle

The Associated Press story would rock the baseball world and sports in general. According to the report, Cobb and his longtime friend and hunting buddy, Tris Speaker, were linked in an investigation being conducted by Commissioner Kenesaw Mountain Landis into an "alleged irregularity" involving a game played in Detroit between the Tigers and the Cleveland Indians on September 25, 1919.

Speaker, like Cobb was a Southerner, born in Hubbard, Texas, and also had been a centerfielder. He racked up more than 3,000 hits in his career and had managed the Indians between 1919 and 1926, taking them to their first World Series title in 1920. Speaker had resigned as manager of the Indians on November 26, just a few days before Cobb resigned from the Tigers, after a similarly glorious career.

Rumors abounded that the two had resigned in an effort to keep their names from being associated with a coming scandal. As the stories played out in the press, it was revealed that former Tigers pitcher Dutch Leonard had given letters written by Cobb and former Indians pitcher/outfielder Joe Wood to American League president Ban Johnson and that these letters proved the two had conspired to fix the 1919 game and that Speaker was in on the fix.

Cobb told reporters it was Leonard and Wood who had bet that Detroit, then in third place, would win against the second-place Indians. Cobb said he didn't know about the bet until long after the game was played, in which Detroit did win, 9–5. Cobb also noted that Wood did not even play in the game; that Speaker—accused of having prior knowledge of a plan for Cleveland to lose—made 3 hits, 2 of which were doubles; and that he himself—accused of knowledge of a prearranged Detroit victory—actually had a lousy day at that particular game getting only 1 hit for the day.

"That ought to show that neither Speaker nor I were in on it," Cobb said. He also told reporters, emotionally, "I have played baseball for 22 years. I couldn't think of anything but win. Every year, every month, every week and every day I did my dead level best to play good baseball and to live so that I could play good ball. I never bet on an American League ball game in my life. I don't believe anybody ever played the game any harder or cleaner or squarer than I.

"I have been involved in this smudge seven years after the thing happened. My position is vindicated in the testimony and so is that of Speaker. I refer the baseball fans of the country to my record in baseball. I am proud of it, and I will leave my case to them."

Cobb and Speaker probably did know the scandal was festering when they resigned as players and managers from their respective teams, but it was by no means clear what had actually happened. Cobb claimed that Leonard's story was so much sour grapes because Cobb had released him from Detroit, and Leonard had refused several offers from Cobb and Speaker to meet them face-to-face in a hearing before Commissioner Landis. The commissioner, after being unable to get Leonard to come meet with him, had gone to Leonard's ranch near Sanger, California, on October 29, 1926, to talk about the matter firsthand.

Cobb, and probably Speaker, was swamped with letters and cards of support with one important telegram being from Fred W. Green, governor-elect of Michigan, and John W. Smith, mayor of Detroit. It read: "We, the undersigned, desire to convey to you the unqualified belief we have in your honesty and integrity and to assure you that we feel your record in baseball is without a blemish. We wish you and your family a merry Christmas and a happy, prosperous New Year."

Along with the governor-elect and mayor were the signatures of various U.S. congressmen and judicial leaders of the area; the board chairman of the Hudson Motor Car Company, and the presidents of both the Packard and Paige motor car companies.

Augustans, as expected, were incredibly supportive with one of the first to speak up being Cobb's own wife, Charlie. "He may have his faults, but dishonesty is not one of them," Mrs. Cobb told local reporters. "I believe that my husband has completely answered the accusations against him, and I only wish to say that I know the charges are untrue in every particular. I know him as no one else does. He has lived clean and played the game clean. He is safe in leaving his case with his friends. To those who know him best the charges are unthinkable."

Federal judge William H. Barrett also led Cobb supporters in saying, "Apart from my general knowledge of Ty Cobb, I particularly recall an experience of several years ago which impressed me very much. It was my duty to take a statement from Cobb involving the reputation of two other baseball players.

"In securing this statement I was deeply impressed with the high plane upon which Cobb placed baseball honor, and how tenacious the players were in keeping it that way. I have known Cobb throughout his baseball career and it is my earnest conviction that he is unquestionably honorable in every particular."

Cobb's hunting friend Dr. E. M. Wilder, secretary of the Georgia Field Trials Association, remarked, "I have known Ty Cobb since he was a lanky youth and have never known him to do a dishonest act. He has lived his life for baseball, and it is ridiculous to believe that he would have jeopardized his brilliant career for a few hundred dollars—or any amount. He is one of the cleanest men I have ever known, absolutely above reproach in matters involving honor."

In Augusta, Cobb invited local newspapermen into the living room of his house on Williams Street and, before a big fireplace, told them his story. According to the *Herald*, "Tears almost welled in his eyes at several junctures of his relation, and many times his voice was shaken and faltering with unashamed feeling."

The *Herald* said Cobb revealed that he and Speaker had been told "in July or August" about Leonard's charges, and Cobb immediately apprised Commissioner Landis of what was happening and demanded a public hearing on the charges. "Speaker and I had nothing to hide in connection with this rotten affair," Cobb further told reporters. "My conscience is clean and clear. . . . Tris Speaker has been in organized baseball for 18 years playing the game as an outstanding man all the time.

"I hold myself up as no paragon, but I have been there for 22 years and have never for a moment been guilty of a dishonorable thought or act, unless it is dishonorable to want to win. If I have committed any wrong, it is that I was too zealous for victory, too anxious to win. I have played the game square and hard continually."

On Christmas Eve of 1926, there was an amazing sight in downtown Augusta as the town's most powerful and wealthiest citizens showed up about 3:30 p.m. for a rally in support of Cobb at the Confederate Monument in the middle of Broad Street. [25] There was Cobb standing on the west side of the monument surrounded by the many speakers braving the cold weather for "Ty Cobb Day." There to the right of the speaker's stand was a large banner that read, WE DON'T BELIEVE IT, TY! And nearby was another large banner that read, YOU'RE STILL THE IDOL OF AMERICA.

"There were many salvos and prolonged cheering when Cobb, his voice vibrant with emotion, and his eyes hinting of tears, rose to address the gathering," the *Chronicle* reported on Christmas Day. "Cobb reiterated his protestations of innocence and spoke in glowing terms of Tris Speaker.

"After touching briefly upon what he termed the 'rotten situation that has sickened me,' Cobb declared that he and Speaker had asked for a verdict, but no verdict was given.

"'There has been a verdict, though,' he concluded. "The way in which the people of America have risen up to declare their disbelief in the charges makes my heart glad.'"

It would be another month before the *Chronicle* proclaimed on January 28, 1927, in a front page headline, LANDIS EXONERATES COBB, SPEAKER. News accounts said Commissioner Landis had set a hearing on the matter to have taken place on January 5, 1927, but again Leonard would not come from California to testify. So, Landis just took no further action except declaring both players to be free agents and making it clear at no time was there ever sufficient concrete evidence to convict Cobb, Speaker, or Wood (who by then had become baseball coach at Yale University).

And in yet another interesting development, *Chronicle* readers were told, "Ban Johnson, the American League president 'now on leave,' had intimated that other evidence was in his possession, but he denied this in a written statement last Sunday night, a few hours before the American League

---

25 Among those present were Judge Barrett, Augusta mayor W. P. White, Richmond County Superior Court judge A. L. Franklin, Chamber of Commerce president L. S. Arrington, Georgia Railroad and Banking Company president Charles H. Phinizy, and many of Cobb's old friends, including Leo F. Cotter, George Conklin, Tom Pilcher, and George Sancken.

club owners took it upon themselves to relieve him of his duties because of ill-health."

The day after that big news, the *Chronicle* would have still another earth-shattering story for baseball fans with a headline reading, TY COBB WILL RETURN TO BASEBALL COMING SEASON FOR 'ONE MORE BIG YEAR.'"

Within a matter of months, Tris Speaker would be wearing the uniform of the Washington Senators and Tyrus R. Cobb would be wearing the uniform of the Philadelphia Athletics.

# THE FINAL RETIREMENT                                    12

ONCE AGAIN TY COBB'S LIFE WAS BEING played out on the front page of the *Augusta Chronicle*. On Wednesday, February 9, 1927, a bold headline that stretched completely from the left side of the top of the front page to the right proclaimed, TY COBB TO PLAY FOR ATHLETICS THIS SEASON. The sub-head told the whole story: CONNIE MACK SECURES STAR FOR $60,000.

This was the same guy the Augusta Tourists had sold for $500 plus, apparently, another $250 for quick delivery. Now he was going to get an amazing salary of $60,000 per year at 1927 prices—the largest salary ever paid a baseball player.[26]

The Associated Press article carried by the *Chronicle* said that Cobb, "former manager of the Detroit Tigers," had announced at a dinner of the Philadelphia Sports Writers on the night of February 8 that he had accepted manager Connie Mack's salary offer. The St. Louis Browns reportedly also had offered Cobb $50,000, according to the story. "Mack and Manager [Dan] Howley, of the St. Louis Browns, made a special trip to

---

26 Just how far Cobb had come is put into perspective by a brief notice the *Chronicle* printed on March 10, 1910, that was reprinted from the *Savannah Evening Press:* "Those of Ty Cobb's friends who wanted him to run for Congress," the notice said, "now see how foolish they were. Ty is to pull down $9,000 a year as a baseball player when a Congressman only gets a measly little seventy-five hundred."

Cobb's home in Augusta, Ga., to lay their offers before him, but the player declined to sign or give either a definite answer until he had considered proposals made by other American league teams."

According to the article, the announcement resulted in a "prolonged cheer" from the sportswriters and other guests in attendance. The article also noted Cobb had been extended the invitation to attend the sportswriters dinner even before he had been cleared of the Dutch Leonard charges as a "vote of confidence" on the part of the Philadelphia sportswriters.

The announcement of Ty Cobb signing with Connie Mack's Philadelphia team met with brotherly love in Augusta as well as the City of Brotherly Love. The *Chronicle*, in an editorial on February 10, 1927, said the reason why "hundreds of thousands of fans would rather see Cobb with Philadelphia than any other team" is because of their "profound admiration for that stalwart Scotsman, Cornelis McGillicudy, who is called Connie Mack for short."

The *Chronicle* editorial summarized, "Ty and Connie match up wonderfully because they are both so clean, so manly, so splendid in every way that the greatest manager in baseball and the greatest player of all times will certainly lead the Athletic to a pennant in 1927.

"Ty Cobb is going to be the greatest drawing card in the history of baseball," the *Chronicle* predicted, "for he has gotten such an enormous amount of publicity because of the unjust attacks made on him that every fan is going to try to see Philadelphia play every time possible, and the $60,000 per year salary that Mack is going to pay him will bring in that astute manager a wonderful harvest in dividends."

In spite of those glowing words, Cobb wasn't even out of spring training with the Athletics in St. Petersburg, Florida, when an incident on March 17, 1927, again earned him some unpleasant headlines. This time, according to the Associated Press, Cobb "in characteristic fashion" during an exhibition game with the Boston Nationals called from the Philadelphia side, "Do you smell anything rotten?" It was unclear, the report said, whether Cobb was directing his remark at the Boston player at bat or umpire Frank Wilson.

Either way, Wilson ordered Cobb from the field, and when Cobb refused to go and was backed up by Athletics coach William J. "Kid" Gleason, umpire Wilson forfeited the game in the fourth inning to the Boston

Braves, which especially was unfortunate since Philadelphia at the time was leading 4–0.[27]

On April 11, 1927, Cobb made his official debut with the Philadelphia Athletics in a game against the Yankees at which Baynard J. Budds, president of the Georgia Society of New York, presented Cobb with a floral horseshoe "as a token of love and appreciation from fellow Georgians."

The same month in Boston, with the season underway, Cobb showed his brilliance playing right field in a hard-fought game against the Red Sox. "Ty Cobb in a Philadelphia uniform was the whole show here today as Connie Mack's rehabilitated Athletics overcame a six run Boston lead to down the Red Sox 9 to 8," the Associated Press related. "The Georgia Peach stole home, drove in two runs, scored twice himself and ended the game with a circus catch and double play unassisted, racing in from the outer garden to catch [Phil] Todt's low fly and double up [William Chester "Baby Doll"] Jacobson at first."

But just about the time the regular season was about to start, something happened that certainly would not be good for Cobb. The owners of the American League clubs resolved whatever differences they had with league president Ban Johnson, and he returned to his Chicago offices after a period of rest in the South. "I never have felt better in the last seven years," he told reporters. "I feel completely restored to health and am ready to return to my duties. For three months, I was a very sick man. I did not realize it until I started on my period of rest."

The Associated Press noted in a story on April 7, "Baseball followers were greatly interested in Johnson's return. He was relieved of his executive duties by the club owners last January, after his clash with Commissioner Landis over the affairs involving Ty Cobb and Tris Speaker.

"It is believed in baseball circles that both Landis and Johnson will be content to call the incident closed."

There certainly had been no love lost between Ty Cobb and Ban Johnson over the years. Their first serious clash had come when Johnson suspended

---

27 Interestingly, Boston club president Judge Emil Fuchs addressed the fans, saying both teams had agreed to play the game again in order not to disappoint the spectators. The replayed game subsequently went seven innings with Boston finally beating Philadelphia, 13–5.

Cobb "indefinitely" from baseball in 1912 for attacking handicapped heckler Claude Lueker in the stands.

Then on May 29, 1922, Cobb was leading the Detroit Tigers in a game against the St. Louis Browns in St. Louis when an argument developed in the ninth inning between manager Cobb and an umpire named Wilson. Cobb stepped on Wilson's toes and was banished from the game and subsequently "suspended indefinitely" by American League President Johnson. Outfielder Harry Heilman also was suspended as a result of the incident.

But just a few days later, on June 2, both were reinstated by Johnson.

On July 17, 1925, Cobb again was "indefinitely suspended" by Johnson due to an argument between Cobb and an umpire named Rowland in the tenth inning of a game between Detroit and Washington. Manager Cobb had protested a strike on Detroit catcher Larry Woodall and was ordered from the field after a short argument. Cobb resumed the quarrel after the game.

Until his suspension was lifted, Cobb had to direct the Tigers from the stands.

Nevertheless, the very next month, on August 30, President Johnson was present in Detroit for a testimonial dinner for Cobb celebrating Cobb's twenty record-breaking years in the American League. The citizens of Detroit that night gave Cobb a $1,000 grandfather clock, and the owners of the Detroit team gave Cobb $10,000.[28]

Cobb emotionally had responded, "Now I see how selfish I have been. My career has been selfish—nothing else. I have done no great good that you should so signally honor me. Oh, why did not I try to do more? Much of what success I may have had has been due in a large measure to the help of others, especially the owners of the Detroit club and the Detroit baseball public."

Just over a year later, Cobb would be saying things not quite so nice about the Detroit club owners for failing to support him fully in the midst of the 1926 scandal. And he certainly wasn't feeling any warm feelings about Johnson for apparently telling reporters that Cobb and Tris Speaker had resigned as player-managers because they saw the handwriting on the wall with the scandal brewing.

---

28 There is a giant photograph of this occasion hanging in the Ty Cobb Museum in Royston, Georgia.

Then, just five months after the scandal and after Johnson's miraculous recovery from his "illness," came another major Cobb–Johnson clash, with Cobb this time wearing the Philadelphia uniform. The incident prompting the clash happened on May 5, in the third of a four-game series between Philadelphia and Boston. Philadelphia had won the first two games.

During the third game, Cobb hit one long and hard over the rightfield fence, but umpire Red Ormsby called it foul. Cobb "bumped" Ormsby in an apparent display of protest, while Al Simmons, a teammate of Cobb's, yelled that the ball was fair. Ormsby subsequently ejected both Cobb and Simmons from the game, which resulted in 8,000 fans pouring onto the field and showering Ormsby with what Johnson later described as "murderous pop bottles."

Local police not only had to escort Ormsby from the ballpark but also had to call for backup officers to handle the angry crowd.

Cobb said the bumping was accidental and apologized to the umpire, but President Johnson said "the point had been conveyed to the crowd of his displeasure over the umpire's decision" and "the mischief had been done."

This wasn't going to be just another ordinary suspension for Cobb, because it would be messing up some very big plans.

Philadelphia was due to play against the Detroit Tigers in Detroit a few days later on May 10, and the city of Detroit was intending to go all out to honor Cobb in his first Detroit "homecoming" game since resigning as the Tigers player-manager the previous November. Fans and undoubtedly higher-up Detroit leaders bombarded Johnson with telegrams urging him to lift his suspension at least so Cobb could play in the game against Detroit and take part in the festivities scheduled to honor him. It probably killed Johnson to do so, because he clearly had not been a fan of Cobb's over the years, but he did relent and lifted the suspension.

That day, Cobb was honored with a testimonial luncheon at noon at the Masonic temple where more than 1,100 persons had places at the tables and another 500 crowded along a balcony railing to observe the proceedings.

"I am grateful to all of you," Cobb said at the luncheon. "You are very kind. It affects me deeply. I am out today in another uniform, but I can't work up the competitive spirit against Detroit. You can't be sold on a town and its people for twenty-two years and then go against them in a competitive way all of a sudden. I have only friendship and gratitude in my heart for the Detroit players and the Detroit fans. I wish to extend my hope that the Detroit club will meet with the greatest success under [new Detroit manager] George Moriarity's leadership."

He then was the featured attraction in a parade to Navin Field led by a police motorcycle escort and a military band. The celebration continued at Navin Field with gift presentation ceremonies and with thousands of fans cheering every time Cobb went to the plate during the game. "The welcoming celebration for the former Detroit manager began shortly after he stepped off a boat from Cleveland with the remainder of the Philadelphia team, and was climaxed shortly before game time with the presentation at the baseball park of an automobile and other gifts," the Associated Press later reported.

And that night he was guest of honor at a dinner sponsored by the Inter-Collegiate Alumni of Detroit in a downtown hotel. It was a great "homecoming," especially since Cobb never would be really at home in Detroit ever again.

In spite of lifting the suspension, the day after the city of Detroit honored Cobb, Johnson not only fined Cobb $200 but also did the same to Cobb's teammate Simmons. Johnson ordered the two Athletics to pay the fines by personal checks within forty-eight hours, meaning that the fines were to be paid directly by the players and not by their club.

And to rub salt in their wounds, Johnson went out of his way to praise Ormsby as being "of the highest type of manhood and of unimpeachable integrity" and pointed out Ormsby's having been honored for distinguished and courageous conduct as a U.S. Marine fighting in the Argonne and Chateau Thierry during World War I. He didn't mention anything about Cobb also having served in France in an army uniform.

Athletics manager Connie Mack responded to Johnson's statement saying the "fair thing" would have been for Johnson to hear both sides of the case before levying the fines. Cobb had said the very same thing about Johnson in 1912 when suspended for attacking handicapped heckler Lueker in the stands. Cobb then complained of the suspension saying, "Johnson has always believed himself to be infallible. He suspends a man first and then investigates afterward. It should be the reverse."

Connie Mack realized the bumping-the-umpire case was not worth the battle and told reporters, "Mr. Johnson is president of the league, and there is no question that he is empowered to make such a ruling. There is nothing left to do but obey it, and the matter will be regarded as a closed affair so far as the Philadelphia club is concerned."

When Ty Cobb started the 1927 season with Philadelphia, he was forty years old, and four months into the season on July 18, 1927, he would get his 4,000th hit, a double in the first inning against Detroit. There would be no other person in all of major league baseball who would match that incredible feat until Pete Rose got his 4,000th hit on April 13, 1984.

Cobb would achieve another interesting record, after turning forty, when he simply hit a typical Cobb home run. Yet that would make Cobb the first professional ballplayer to hit a home run in a major-league game before he was twenty and after he was forty. (The only other player, at this writing, to duplicate that feat is Rusty Staub.[29])

All good things must come to an end, and Cobb once again thought his playing days had ended when, in November of 1927, fresh from a hunting trip out west, he met with Athletics manager Connie Mack in Philadelphia for a salary discussion but failed to reach an agreement on a new contract.

"Cobb came to us last season under a very heavy contract, and we feel that we are unable to continue the high salary next year," Mack later told reporters in referring to Cobb's $60,000 fee for playing for the Athletics. "I am very sorry that we will lose him. He is a great player. We liked him on the club. We liked his playing and would like to keep him."

The Georgia Peach himself made no definite statement as to his intentions, but observed he had been playing in the major leagues for twenty-three seasons and was thinking of the time when he would retire. Apparently, the *Augusta Chronicle* thought it was a done deal because on November, 3, 1927, it head-lined, COBB WILL NOT PLAY WITH A'S NEXT YEAR; LEAVES FOR AUGUSTA.

---

29 Staub, a native of New Orleans, Louisiana, played twenty-three seasons in the major leagues (1963–1985) for the Houston Colt .45s and Astros, Montreal Expos, New York Mets, Detroit Tigers, and Texas Rangers.

Cobb returned to Augusta with the *Chronicle* running a stock photo of him with a baseball bat headlined, Ty Cobb Home Again. The brief caption under the photo said, "Ty Cobb, the peerless star of the diamond has returned to Augusta to spend the winter at home. He and Connie Mack having agreed that the Athletics cannot pay him what he wants next season, the star announced upon reaching Augusta that, although he wouldn't say definitely, he probably has played his last baseball game."

The caption continued, "Although many of his friends are urging him to return to the diamond next season, Cobb says it is not likely that he will ever wield another bat on the big league diamonds. He will not make a definite announcement as to his future plans for several weeks."

But Cobb's playing days were not over, and that may have been due to a very interesting thing that had happened a few months earlier. Ban Johnson—Cobb's nemesis—retired as American League president on October 17, 1927, after heading the league he started for its first twenty-eight years. Cobb's old boss, Tigers president Frank Navin, was named acting president of the American League. It's very possible Cobb's lifelong competitive nature made him want to play at least one season more without Ban Johnson hovering over him. It's also very possible Cobb's admiration of and long friendship with Connie Mack made him back off his contract demands. In late March, just as spring training camps were opening, Cobb let an *Augusta Herald* reporter, most likely Earl Bell, in on a big secret: He had decided to play another season with the Athletics.

The *Herald* broke the news to local fans and the world in general on the afternoon of Friday, March 30, 1928, with a headline stretching completely across the top of its front page, Ty Cobb Denies Story That He Is Quitting.

A story had circulated that Cobb had made a $200,000 profit in the stock market, and that windfall had led him to decide to end his baseball career for good. "I wish it were true that I had made such a clean up," Cobb told a *Herald* reporter "but even it were so, it would have no bearing on my playing this year. . . . My playing with the Athletics this year has no connection with my financial standing. I have given Connie Mack my word to play this year, and I'm going to play with the Athletics."

The *Herald* also reported Cobb had come home to Augusta a few days earlier because his wife, Charlie, required a minor operation. "Mrs. Cobb is in the care of a very dear friend in Royston, Ga., where the operation was performed," he said, very likely referring to his childhood friend, Dr. Stewart Brown. "She is getting along well, and I came back to Augusta this morning to get the children and take them to see their mother. If Mrs. Cobb continues to improve, I will leave Monday to join the Athletics."

The *Chronicle* ran an article the next morning by Brian Bell that read, in part: "[Cobb] had determined in the winter season to retire but was persuaded by Manager Mack to 'play one more year,'" noting Cobb had hit .357 the previous season and finished fifth in the American League playing against much younger men.

"Nevertheless, it is a tired Ty starting out on his 24th year as a major leaguer," the reporter observed. "The years have made him weary of baseball and its traveling far from home. The game's first playing millionaire does not need the money and he has begun to fear he may break his legs along with the record, but he is still willing to take the chance.

"When he retires for good, it will be for the good of opposing pitchers who have been giving cheers as word came of his exit, only to recall them when Ty says, 'not yet.'"

The 1928 season for Cobb opened with the Athletics playing the New York Yankees in Philadelphia. It was special because it not only marked the start of Cobb's twenty-fourth season but also the debut of Tris Speaker, formerly of the Washington Senators, wearing an Athletics uniform.

Fans must have been anxious to see the former opposing player-managers, who endured the 1926 scandal, now playing on the same team, because an estimated 20,000 shivering fans braved bitter cold with the Athletics unfortunately losing their season opener, 8–5. Cobb had managed to hit a single at his first time back at bat in the new season, but Speaker failed to hit safely in his debut.

Still, there would be many more games ahead for both to pick up speed.

On June 15 in the eighth inning of a game against the Indians in Cleveland, Cobb stole home, contributing to the Athletics victory over the Indians, 12–5. That would mark the fifty-fourth time Cobb had made a clean steal of home and also the last time he did that in regular season major-league play.

Ty Cobb's final game in professional baseball would not be a pretty or an honorable ending to his legendary career. The Athletics lost the third game in a crucial series to the New York Yankees, on the Yankees home turf on September 11, 1928. The victory all but gave the Yankees the American League title.

Lou Gehrig was on second in the eighth inning when the mighty George Herman "Babe" Ruth came up to bat. The first ball from Philadelphia pitcher Bob Grove led Ruth to try a bunt, which went foul past the third baseline. The next pitch was called a ball. Then, magic happened with Ruth making solid contact on Grove's third pitch. The ball sailed into the rightfield bleachers and earned Ruth home run number 49. The park full of 40,000 spectators turned into bedlam. Associated Press writer William J. Chipman noted that Athletics manager Connie Mack "was visibly shaken by the blast which shattered his dreams of a baseball empire."

In the ninth inning, Athletics players Cobb, Eddie Collins, and Wally French each came up to the home plate, and each was put out in succession by a young Yankees pitcher from Florida named Henry Johnson. "The first two of those names [Cobb and Collins], as names alone, would have been enough to frighten the average young pitcher out of the box as recently as two years ago," reporter Chipman noted, "but not Johnson today."

Cobb was put out by Johnson "on a hoist" to shortstop Mark Anthony Koening. Collins was out on a foul fly "to the same gentleman of the defense," and French was out on a pop fly to leftfielder Bob Meusel. With that the Yankees won 5–3, and the greatest ballplayer in the world walked off a major-league playing field for what would be his final time.

Six days after that final game, Cobb again told reporters on Monday, September 17, 1928, he was through with professional baseball. "Guess it's time to get out of the game and play with my kids before they grow up and leave me," he said. "And there's that trip to Europe that I promised Mrs. Cobb this year."

Did the fans and reporters really believe him this time?

He still was playing a great game of ball—playing in ninety-five regular season games in the 1928 season, racking up 353 times at bat, getting 114 hits, scoring 54 runs, with 1 home run, and ending the season with a .323 batting average.

On top of that sports fans and sportswriters had been down that Looks-Like-I'm-Quitting Road at last three times before: The first had been after his army service, which was really a coy game to get him a better contract in returning to the Tigers. The second quitting announcement came when he and Tris Speaker retired as player-managers in 1926. The third came in 1927 when Connie Mack said Philadelphia couldn't afford his $60,000 salary, and Cobb indicated maybe his playing days were through. And, now the fourth time had come with Cobb contending he was just "baseball tired."

The *Chronicle* apparently also wasn't totally convinced knowing Cobb's had poor-mouthed before of how "tired" he was only to come back with another great year, still apparently drinking that Nuxated Iron stuff he had endorsed. Probably because they weren't sure, *Chronicle* editors put Cobb's latest announcement of his retirement on the second page and not the front as it had for so many other major events in Cobb's life.

Still, the *Chronicle* couldn't help but remark fondly, "The memory of Cobb, on the eve of his departure from the game, goes back to August 26, 1905, when he joined the Detroit Tigers. With the opening of the 1907 season, he became the greatest all around player in the history of the pastime. He continued to lead until he took over the managing end of the Detroit club when Hughie Jennings dropped as far as his major league playing days were concerned.

"I will be leaving baseball with a lot of regrets," he told reporters, "and still with a light heart. It's hard to pull away from a game to which one has given a quarter century of his best manhood and which paved the road to lift me to a place of prominence and affluence."

But, in spite of all of his "poor-me" talk about how tired he was from playing baseball, barely a month after officially calling it quits he went to play baseball in Japan!

# CAN'T GET AWAY FROM
# THE GAME 13

AFTER THE 1928 SEASON ENDED, Cobb was barely back home in Augusta when he confirmed a report he would leave in a few days for Japan to join a team of major-league players to take on a Japanese ball team.

According to the *Chronicle,* he would sail on October 24, 1928, and return to the United States in mid-December. As it turned out, Cobb was the only major-league player on the trip with G. H. Putnam, co-owner of the San Francisco Seals of the Pacific Coast League and a good friend of Cobb, going along for the ride. Also on the trip were Charlie Cobb and the family's three youngest children: Jimmie, Beverly, and Herschel.

"While in Japan, Cobb will don the uniforms of four university nines—Keio, Waseda, Meiji and Osaka—at various times playing in actual competitions with other teams," the *Chronicle* related. "Ten or more games will be played. The four institutions and the newspaper Mainichi Shimbun are sponsoring the trip."

Photos of that trip show Cobb towering over Japanese players and wearing a pre-World War II baseball uniform with "Tokyo" in bold, black letters across his chest.

The travelers expected to return by way of China, Manila, and Honolulu before arriving back in San Francisco by Christmas. Christmas of 1928 passed quietly for Cobb and his family with reporters occasionally inquiring as to Cobb's true intentions about giving up baseball for good as a player.

On February 9, 1929, the *Chronicle* headlined, COBB REITERATES DECISION To QUIT, with the article noting that Cobb was resisting heading for any Florida big-league training camp. Cobb told reporters, "I said I was going to retire while I was still the Georgia Peach and not a has been, and I meant it."

The newspaper noted Cobb was recuperating at his home from a mild attack of influenza. The article added, "He has promised his family a trip to Europe this year and possibly will be off in the Spring while the men he has worked with in his prime are hooking up their harness in Florida for another season."

Meanwhile, Augustans were told on February 17, the Baltimore Orioles of the International League planned to bring thirty to thirty-five players to Augusta in early March for spring training. The players would be staying at the Richmond Hotel on Broad Street. Lester Moody, secretary of the Augusta Chamber of Commerce, was working out the details with club officials; the club would train at the Municipal Stadium rather than the old Warren Park.

As expected, the Orioles did come to town along with their new manager, Fritz Maisel, former New York Yankees star. "The warm sun of this Southern city is working like a magic spell on the Baltimore Orioles, who showed unusually good form yesterday in their second work-out in camp," the *Chronicle* related. "Manager Maisel, during the two hitting sessions, gave all his pitchers in the camp an opportunity to release the winter kinks. Those who pitched to the batters included James Boswell, William Runge, Ray Walker, John Hollingsworth, John Wisner, Howard Cates and Fred Combs, the 'old veteran.'"

Besides the other Orioles, who turned out for the spring training on March 12, 1929, the famous Augusta resident made an appearance at the field: "The Oriole candidates during the afternoon session were paid a visit by Ty Cobb, the Georgia Peach, who gave the rookies a few expert lessons in hitting," the *Chronicle* noted. "The ex-Tiger star showed the youngsters the proper stand at the plate, how to grip the bat and a few more of the rudiments of hitting."

The next week the *Chronicle* published a photo of Cobb and a Baltimore player with the caption reading, "Ty Cobb, the greatest of them all, donned his uniform once more to work out with the Baltimore Orioles here last week. The Georgia Peach is shown here giving a few batting pointers to Don Heffner, 17-year-old second baseman of the Orioles."[30]

Cobb must have enjoyed his workout with the Orioles and must have been given his due respect, because he was back on the field with them when they resumed practice in Augusta in May after playing some exhibition games.

The *Chronicle* reported on May 19, "Ty Cobb, the Georgia Peach, was out for the workout and except for a little excess weight looked like the same inimitable Cobb of old. He took his regular turn at the bat, slamming hits to all corners of the park and fielded a few besides."

Apparently, Cobb was there because of his love for the game and the love for his hometown, because he intentionally had made himself unavailable for other offers, according to syndicated cartoonist and writer Quin Hall. "Undoubtedly Cobb hated to quit the game," Hall wrote in an article printed in the *Chronicle* on May 31, 1929. "He could have hooked up with several clubs, but he kept the figure for his services at such a high point that the club owners balked. Dan Howley, the explosive manager of the St. Louis Browns, wanted Ty to do a little pinch hitting with his gang. When Owner [Philip] Ball was told the salary the Peach expected, negotiations ended pronto. So the game goes on without the immortal Cobb." Hall also noted missing from major-league lineups was for the first time since 1908 the "silver-haired outfielder" Tris Speaker, although he was still active in baseball as manager of the Newark International club.

By the fall of 1929, Cobb apparently was having a bad attack of separation pains, because the *Chronicle* published a teasing headline on October 4 saying, COBB WILL RETURN TO GAME, HE SAYS. Cobb told reporters in New York City that he still was holding to his personal pledge

---

30 Actually, Heffner of Rouzerville, Pennsylvania, had turned eighteen just the month before. Still, you wonder what Cobb was thinking while talking to that player who was about the same age that Cobb was when he joined the Augusta Tourists a quarter of a century earlier. Here was Cobb at the end of his playing career with a teenager just starting out on his.

not to play pro ball again, but was considering offers to be a club executive or possibly even a manager again.

"The executive end of the game has the most appeal to me now," he said. "I am not ready to say that I would not manage a club again, although, of course, I shall never play again. The idea of a major league connection in an advisory connection appeals to me most.

"I have found that you can not spend 24 years in baseball and then forget it unless you do as I did and go a long way off. I have not felt a yearning for the game this summer, because I was in Europe and there was no baseball all about me as there would have been if I had stayed at home, but now that I am back, it is different.

"Tentative offers have been made, and I believe I will be back in the game next year. I would prefer an executive job rather than active management for the manager is too good a mark to shoot at. He's out where a sharpshooter can hardly miss if he wants to fire a shot. The executive can hide in his office or get under the stands. However, I never thought I was such a bad manager as many people thought. When I retired from active play, I followed a program I had mapped out long ago. I said then that they never would have to cut my uniform to make me quit, and I would get out when I thought the proper time had come. The time came, and I retired.

"Now I feel that I can come back in another angle of the game, and I think now I shall. It's a great game. I love it. It has been good to me, and probably I'll be back in it again soon. If I make a connection, it'll be in the majors. I have had not minor league offers, and I'm not interested except in the majors."

The article noted Cobb would head for Philadelphia and then on to Chicago to attend the 1929 World Series where he would be a "baseball reporter."[31]

---

31 At the Augusta Museum of History this author came across an interesting photo taken at the World Series. It shows Cobb lined up in a pose with Babe Ruth, Connie Mack, Commissioner Kenesaw Mountain Landis, and other World Series celebrities. The photo is autographed to Cobb from Christy Walsh "Senior" with the inscription saying, "Best Wishes to good old Tyrus who 'covered' the 1929 World Series with our other 'big shots.'" Walsh was the business manager for Lou Gehrig and Babe Ruth and was known for making commercial sports deals. The reason he wrote the word covered in quotes is because he was known to have contracted with newspapers and magazines to have articles "written" by sports stars when in reality they were authored by professional writers working for Walsh.

Sitting and watching the final game of the 1929 World Series on October 14, at Shibe Park in Philadelphia, must have been tough on Cobb, who himself had never been on a winning World Series team.

In the ninth inning of the fifth and deciding game of the 1929 World Series Connie Mack's men surged from behind to score three runs and beat the Chicago Cubs, champions of the National League, 3–2. "No other manager in baseball has ever won four world's series," the Associated Press reported. "This was Mack's fourth in six tries since 1905, adding 1929 to the other victorious years of 1910, 1911, and 1913. John McGraw is the only other living man who has won as many as three world's titles, the mark which the late Miller Huggins also attained with the Yankees."

Cobb's spirits were lifted back home in Augusta when he got together with an amazing mix of professional and amateur baseball players on the afternoon of October 27, 1929, at the Lenwood Hospital baseball diamond, for a game sponsored by the local post of the American Legion.

Cobb and Bob Dressel of Augusta served as umpires for the benefit game.

The *Chronicle* observed: "When Cobb first came to Augusta in the early 1900s and played the outfield at old Warren Park, Mr. Dressel, the late Leo Cotter, and other fans, were Cobb's greatest boosters and all lived to see the peerless Cobb become one of the game's greatest players. Mr. Dressell and Cobb remained friends since those days when the Georgia Peach was just another gangling ball player from the sticks."

The "visiting team" for the game at the Lenwood Hospital baseball diamond included "Rabbit" Whitney from the Montreal club; George Ferrell, Memphis; Wesley Ferrell, Cleveland; Rick Ferrell, St. Louis Browns; Tom Zachary, New York Yankees; Alvin Crowder, St. Louis Browns; Fred Mooney, Atlanta; Johnny Jones, Charlotte; Sam Hanley, Springfield; and Jim Poole, Nashville.

The "home team" included Harry Smythe, Philadelphia Nationals; Marian Smythe, Augusta; Roy Spencer, Washington; Luke Williams, Augusta; Tripp Sigman, Philadelphia Nationals; J. C. Hardy, Augusta; Virgin Steele, cleanup man for the University of Georgia the previous season; and local players Peterson, Peters, Anderson, Trommerhauser, Johansen, Smoak, Cox, Herman, and Moog.

About 500 people were on hand to watch the team of big leaguers and some players from minor leagues beat the local team, 10–3.

The *Chronicle* described the two main pitchers, writing, "Harry Smythe, Augustan, who last season became one of Bert Shotton's leading pitchers with the Phillies, was in the box for the locals during the first half of the game and held the visiting big leaguers to one run while he was twirling. Peters and Cox, local amateurs, took turns in the box after Smythe retired.

"Wes Ferrell, ace of the Cleveland Indians, pitched part of the game for the big leaguers, while Alvin Crowder of the St. Louis Browns finished the game. The three Ferrell boys—Wes, Rick and George—all were in the lineup." [32]

Throughout 1930, Ty Cobb was popping in and out of the Augusta newspapers for a variety of activities, most of them having nothing at all to do with baseball. His hopes or intentions of becoming an executive with a major-league baseball team were quickly fading.

On February 10, Pathe News photographed Cobb and well-known players Eddie Collins and "Ernie" Earnshaw hunting on the Allen Jones estate near Magruder, Georgia, in Burke County, apparently near Cobb's own hunting preserve. Collins was with the Philadelphia Athletics and would retire after the 1930 season. Reporting on this affair, the *Chronicle* noted, "The celebrities have been entertained with a dinner and opossum hunt by Sim Bell, president of the Georgia Field Trials association, who was on the grounds with them today. The players have visited Waynesboro on their sojourn in the confines of Burke County."

---

32 Actually there were seven Ferrell brothers from North Carolina as detailed in the book *The Ferrell Brothers of Baseball* by Dick Thompson. Rick Ferrell would retire after catching 1,806 games. He would play for the St. Louis Browns, Boston Red Sox, and Washington Senators before being inducted into the Baseball Hall of Fame in 1984. His brother, Wes, almost as famous as Ty Cobb for his volatile temper, was a great pitcher who played for the Cleveland Indians, Boston Red Sox, Washington Senators, New York Yankees, Brooklyn Dodgers, and Boston Braves. On July 19, 1933, Rick playing for the Red Sox and Wes playing for the Indians made baseball history as brothers on opposing teams each hitting homers in the same game.

Cobb was the main speaker at the City Basketball League's banquet on April 3, held for the players on the basketball teams sponsored by Friedman Jewelers, Farr and Hogan, Augusta Sporters, Auto Top and Tire Company, Bowen Brothers, and the Georgia Power Company. Tickets had been given to the managers of the teams to distribute to the players upon request.

Earlier that same week, on March 31, 1930, Cobb was among the guests at a banquet in the Bon Air-Vanderbilt Hotel near Cobb's house given by hotel manager A. E. Martin in honor of sportswriter Grantland Rice and golfer Bobby Jones, who was playing that week at the Augusta Country Club in the first Southeastern Open Golf Tournament.

Many years later, the *Augusta Chronicle*'s sports editor Ward Clayton would write, "In the early days of the Masters Tournament, Bobby Jones would stand on the hill overlooking the 11th green and 12th tee at Augusta National Golf Club and point toward the ninth fairway of the adjacent Augusta Country Club. 'That's where I played my finest golf in 1930,' Jones would say as he pointed beyond the tall pines behind the 12th green and 13th tee of Augusta National.

"It was a big boast, considering 1930 was the year of Jones' miraculous Grand Slam, when he won the U.S. Open and Amateur and the British Open and Amateur. [Today's Grand Slam consists of all professional events—the Masters, U.S. Open, British Open and PGA Championship.] Jones played in two other events that year. In one of them he demolished a strong field at the Southeastern Open in Augusta, the town that four years later would play host to the first Masters on the course that Jones built, Augusta National.

"The Southeastern Open, held in 1930 and 1931 with 36 holes each at the Augusta Country Club and the nearby Forrest Hills-Ricker course, was not directly related to the Masters, but it played a part in its birth.

"When Jones announced in 1931 the purchase of The Fruitlands Nursery, land that would become Augusta National, he said, 'My experience in this city, in the Southeastern Open Championship last spring, convinced me that nowhere in this hemisphere is there anything to surpass the golf conditions, in turf, greens, or climate, offered by this immediate locality.'"

Just a few days after the Southeastern Open, on April 24, Cobb was in Columbia, South Carolina, for both the opening of the new Columbia airport and to toss out the first ball opening the 1930 season of the South Atlantic League. The trip must have held a lot of memories for Cobb since the Columbia Skyscrapers team was the first-ever professional ball club Cobb played against on the first day of the South Atlantic League's existence twenty-six years to the month earlier. He had played two games against Columbia at Warren Park in Augusta before being dropped by the Tourists before the team's third game against the Skyscrapers, played in Columbia.

"The people in the South Carolina capital are looking forward to seeing Ty Cobb at the first game, as the famous star has not honored Columbia with an official visit in many years, and there are thousands of people who have not seen him since he severed his connection with the great American game which hoisted him to the pinnacle of fame," observed *Chronicle* writer Bob Parks in his "Grin 'n Bare It" column.

The columnist then sort of rubbed it in, noting, "We folks in Augusta see Ty almost daily around town, at the ball park, the golf course and the basketball game, and most of us know him personally, but it is quite an occasion when such a famous figure in the sports world appears in public in a city which hasn't seen him in several years."

Cobb was sitting in the guest box with South Carolina governor John G. Richards when the governor's granddaughter, Jane Todd of Laurens, South Carolina, broke a bottle of champagne dedicating the airport in honor of Columbia mayor L. B. Owens.

On April 26, the *Chronicle* published a photo showing the South Carolina governor standing next to Cobb as the retired player threw out the first ball opening the 1930 SALLY League season. The headline over the photo almost wistfully proclaimed, Ty Cobb Back in the Game.

Baseball was changing faster than even Cobb probably imagined. During the next month, in Des Moines, Iowa, a crowd of 12,000 watched the first night baseball game played under permanent lights, as the Des Moines team played a club from Wichita, Kansas, in the Western League, on May 2, 1930.

Just barely over two months later, the Augusta Wolves—as the town's minor-league team was then known—hosted what is said to be the first professional baseball game in the South played under permanent lights, with the Wolves being beaten 5–3 by the Charlotte (North Carolina) Hornets on July 19, at the Municipal Stadium in Allen Park, off Walton Way.

"The opening night game saw approximately 5,000 fans in the grandstand and bleachers, many who were there to watch the game while many others came merely to see what night baseball looked like," wrote *Chronicle* reporter John F. Battle Jr. "They were rewarded in seeing a game played as if by daylight. Both from a financial standpoint and baseball, the new venture was a success. It was the opinion of many that night baseball is here to stay, and [club] President Marvin Wolfe has at last found an amusement that will satisfy those thousands who ride about at night seeking some attraction out of the ordinary."

By mid-December of 1930, Cobb had settled into retirement in Augusta and even had accepted the general chairmanship of the newly formed Augusta Sports Committee, an advertising branch of the Augusta Chamber of Commerce. Besides Cobb were thirty-two other members including such prominent citizens as Dr. W. D. Jennings, Fielding Wallace, Stewart Phinizy, George Ricker, George Claussen, Thomas Barrett Jr., W. H. Lanier, and Cobb's longtime newspaper supporter, Thomas J. Hamilton.

About the same time Cobb agreed to be general chairman of the Augusta Sports Committee, he was celebrating his forty-fourth birthday. "The famous Georgia Peach, after twenty years in major league baseball, has laid down his war club for the golf stick and shot gun, and is probably finished with baseball unless something extraordinary turns up to lure him back to the national sport," the *Herald* noted on December 20.

Sounding like sour grapes, Cobb complained to the *Herald* reporter, "To me, the game seems to lack spontaneity now. The close plays, base running and other interesting features have been lessened by the orgy of home run hitting.

"Back before the days of the lively ball, the outfielders played nearer the infield and figured in some fast throws and hair-line decisions. The present game needs more competition, more close scores and harder fought games. The lively ball has served to eliminate some of the attractive points.

"Years ago, I remember when crowded stands greeted a seventh place club late in September. They were out to see real baseball, with all the old tricks of the game. Nowadays only the leaders are the first division clubs play to full stands. The others have meager attendance."

At the close of December of 1930, the local newspaper ran a photo of Cobb bird hunting with his shotgun with the photo captioned tongue in cheek, TY COBB IS NOW CHASING FOWLS.

Little did Cobb know just how foul the next year of 1931 would be for him and his family.

# TROUBLE IN THE
# COBB HOUSEHOLD                                    14

IF THE STOCK MARKET CRASH of October 24, 1929, that ushered in the Great
Depression had any effect on Tyrus Raymond Cobb's financial fortunes, there
was little indication by the lifestyle he continued to enjoy during his retirement years. The first week of 1931 saw the Augusta Polo and Racing Club
selecting its president, M. W. Partridge of the Partridge Inn hotel and restaurant, other officers, and its board of directors, which included Ty Cobb.

Cobb was apparently game for just about anything in his early retirement years with one of the strangest being an "aerial golf game" reported in
the *Chronicle* on January 27, 1931: "In the first aerial golf game ever held
here, Ty Cobb and Dave Ogilvie Jr. tied with Dr. William Lyon Phelps,
Lampson professor of English at Yale, and Charley Gray, golf pro," the
*Chronicle* reported. "The match was played at the Municipal course, and the
scores were 27 each for nine holes.

"Ogilvie and Gray were in the planes and, as they dropped the balls as
close to the greens as possible, Dr. Phelps and Cobb played them in. On
number four hole, Ogilvie placed a ball on the edge of the green and Dr.
Phelps was in in two. This is a par four hole. The planes were flying at an
altitude of 500 feet and every ball dropped fell within fifty feet of the greens.
A gallery of 200 or more persons witnessed the unique contest."

In late February and early March, Cobb played in the Bon Air-Vanderbilt Hotel–sponsored golf tournament held at the Augusta Country Club. He defeated Tom Summerville of Wilmington, Delaware, in the second round. Cobb's final round match with former Augusta mayor Raleigh H. Daniel had to be postponed on the last day of February because of rain and was rescheduled for March 1.

It was reported both Daniel and Cobb had been shooting in the eighties throughout the week. That final day of play, Cobb won the hotel's tournament.

The first week of March found Cobb speaking about baseball to the Augusta Kiwanis Club at the Hotel Richmond (where the Albion Hotel once stood). And just two days after that, the *Chronicle* carried the news that the old grandstand at Warren Park had been demolished because Warren Park had become an "inconvenient location" for baseball and the city had built a better municipal stadium beside the Augusta Canal at Allen Park off Walton Way between 13th and 15th Streets.

The newspaper noted the old grandstand was not exactly the same as when Cobb played with the Tourists and when he brought exhibition teams to Augusta, but that some of the same timbers had been used in its rebuilding stages. "H. D. Horton, who demolished the old grandstand," the *Chronicle* related, "has completed his work but, before he did so, he telephoned Ty Cobb and told him that he would save him a piece of the original timbers from which he may make some home utensil or perhaps even a wooden desk decoration as a memento of the days when the fleet Georgian, then about 17 years of age, burned up the South Atlantic league with Andy Roth as his mentor and guide."

Everything seemed fine in Cobb's life of retirement bliss until . . . the *Chronicle* told readers the Cobbs' marriage was falling apart with a headline on Thursday, April 16, 1931, that said, MRS. TYRUS R. COBB SUES FOR DIVORCE, followed by a subhead, CRUEL TREATMENT ALLEGED; WIFE ASKS CUSTODY OF CHILDREN.

According to the article, Mrs. Cobb had filed a suit for divorce and was seeking permanent alimony through her attorneys, Hammond & Kennedy, with the petition to be heard April 25 before Judge A. L. Franklin of the

Superior Court. Mrs. Cobb's attorneys were former judge Henry C. Hammond[33] and future judge of the Superior Court F. Frederick Kennedy. The latter also was the county government attorney at the time he was representing Mrs. Cobb. The petition for divorce, as quoted by the *Chronicle*, contended "That defendant has inflicted upon plaintiff cruel treatment within the meaning of the law and of such character as to warrant a total divorce" and "that she be awarded the custody of said minor children."

(The *Chronicle* reported the Cobbs as having five children and listed them as Tyrus Raymond Cobb Jr., 21; Shirley M., 19; R. Herschel, 14; Beverly, 11; and Howell [Jimmy], 9.)

For the average Augustan or most any baseball fan in the nation, that news must have come as a total surprise. There were no scandal magazines to speak of in those days and certainly no syndicated "entertainment" television shows that exploited bad news about celebrities. The Augusta newspapers, up until this time, has not written anything about Cobb's marital life that indicated there were any trouble between him and his wife.

Many Augustans, however, were not stupid and had heard rumors or knew firsthand of Cobb's marital problems and his physical cruelty to his wife and children. Charlie's niece, Elna Anne Lombard, daughter of Charlie's brother, Roswell Lombard, would tell this author, "I remember he cut her [Charlie] with a knife once. The little finger on her right hand always was bent after that. . . . He was a mean SOB."

Billy Calhoun, the late Augusta attorney and former city councilman, who had played tennis against Ty Jr., also told this author, "My father, Frank, who was a cotton broker, owned Bunny Hall Plantation near Yemessee, South Carolina. Cobb came to hunt there, and they became fast friends. He was a good shot and very competitive at hunting like he was at baseball. I had hanging in my bedroom a baseball that all the Detroit Tigers autographed including him. I don't know what happened to that baseball.

"After Cobb moved from Augusta, my father hosted a seated dinner at our home every fall for Cobb and his close friends. He was a very affable,

---

33 Hammond was one of those who stood up for Cobb at the Confederate Monument in Augusta on Christmas Eve of 1926 during the baseball scandal.

polite gentleman," Calhoun added. "There was no evidence of him being anything but a perfect gentleman. He was definitely a man's man, loved and liked by the men who knew him. But he was rough on his children, and I don't think women liked him for the way he treated his wife."

Someone in the know might have caught a double meaning in the words of Charlie Cobb when the 1926 baseball scandal broke. Remember, she specifically had told reporters, "He may have his faults, but dishonesty is not one of them. . . . I know him as no one else does."

As mentioned earlier Cobb's oldest daughter, Shirley, admitted, "I never spent five seconds with that man that I wasn't scared pea green. He beat everybody, and we weren't bad children."

Cobb ruled his household when he was home with the same toughness that umpires ruled the playing fields during Cobb's playing career. The difference was the umpires would never hit Cobb like Cobb would hit his wife and kids. He came from that old method of raising children: "Spare the rod and spoil the child." His youngest daughter, Beverly, told this author, "He was a very driven man. He had a difficult time with anyone not willing to put out their best to excel, and that made him a difficult parent."

When asked if she knew when the alienation started between Cobb and his wife and children, Beverly replied, "The alienation started as long as I can remember. It was an unhappy home. My mother was home all of the time, and he had to be away. He was a law unto himself. He made his own laws. . . . All I remember is when he came home he did a lot of hunting and golfing. I do not remember him taking me out to lunch or a play or that kind of thing. He took the boys hunting, and he adored my sister [Shirley]."

Cobb was in California attending the opening of the San Francisco baseball club's new Seal Stadium when he got the news of his wife seeking a divorce and was with Harry Lea, the "Richmond County tobacco man." They were guests of George Putnam of the San Francisco Seals, who had been with Cobb on his trip to Japan. "Naturally I am surprised and shocked," the Associated Press quoted Cobb as saying. "I do not know what to say except that I have always loved my wife, my children and my home. I am sorry such apparently hasty action as this was taken in my absence from my home and without having consulted me in the matter.

"A family is an institution where the children's interests should come first, and even now I say that Mrs. Cobb and I should think of our children and not bring them into any court procedure."

Following her filing for divorce, Charlie apparently took advantage of Cobb being out of town and moved her and the kids out of the big, two-story house on Williams Street. The 1932 City of Augusta directory lists Charlie and her children living at 1122 Greene Street (now a vacant lot just east of the Greyhound bus station). It was while living at the Greene Street address a horrible incident happened to further give Charlie Lombard Cobb immense grief.

About 9:00 p.m. on Monday, June 27, 1932, fifteen-year-old Herschel Cobb and a twenty-six-year-old popular Augusta entertainer named Tommy Hankins were in Spellman's Alley in the rear of the house where Cobb, his mother, and siblings were living. Cobb was helping Hankins pour gasoline into Hankins's car. Who knows what he was thinking—maybe to see better in the dark alley—but Cobb lit a match near the gas tank that ignited the gasoline and set Hankins's clothes on fire. Hankins was burned severely on his arms, legs, shoulders, and back, and nearly all of his clothes were burned from his body as he ran from the scene.

The *Chronicle* reported, "Some unidentified person helped to extinguish the blaze and rushed him to the hospital where for three days he fought gamely but vainly for his life." Hankins died at University Hospital on June 30, and he was buried the next day in Westover Cemetery after a funeral service at First Baptist Church, then located downtown at Eighth and Greene Streets, a few blocks from where the tragedy had occurred.

Herschel Cobb, who was not burned, was listed among the honorary pallbearers.

Hankins had been a salesman at Friedmans Jewelry store and was active with the Baptist Young People's Union at First Baptist. He was prominent in local stage productions as a dancer and comedian with his last appearance being at the Masonic Festival in Hephzibah, Georgia, near Augusta.

"Hundreds of automobiles lined both sides of Greene Street for two blocks," the *Chronicle* reported of the funeral service, "and a host of friends and admirers packed the church to capacity."

Several months after the incident, Hankins's mother, Sarah, filed a $10,000 suit against Herschel Cobb and his mother, charging Mrs. Cobb had directed her son to take gasoline out of her car and put it in the car driven by Hankins, and, that in doing this, he was acting as the agent of Mrs. Cobb. However, on March 22, 1933, a Richmond County Superior Court jury deliberated for two hours and returned a not guilty verdict in favor of the defendants.

There could have been any number of reasons why Charlie decided to drop her divorce suit against Ty. She did, and sometime in 1932—not long after the fire death of Tommy Hankins—the Cobbs moved from Georgia to California; settling twenty-two miles south of San Francisco in a Spanish-style, fifteen-room (seven bedrooms) mansion at 48 Spencer Lane in Atherton.

When Cobb's younger daughter, Beverly McLaren, was asked why the family moved to California, she replied, "My brother [Jimmy] was a premature child. They didn't expect him to live. He was full of heat rash. He had the colic. The doctors said maybe if he could be in a milder climate, there might be a chance. The first night in California, my mother said was the first time Jimmy slept more than four hours. Jimmy is now sixty."[34]

Cobb's other daughter, Shirley Beckworth, told this author her parents were separated for nineteen months in Georgia before they moved to California, and she actually had tried to keep them from getting back together. "I was the stinker that kept them apart," she said. "I didn't want them to go back together, because I thought it would be more of the same. Leopards don't change their spots. They got back together, though, for the move. They thought things would be different. They had some kind of peculiar love. I didn't understand it, and I don't want to understand it. They sacrificed for the children [to give them a home], but I really didn't have a home. You don't run away from a home. You run to it."

As Cobb became more and more acclimated to his new California home, he also became more and more philosophical about his past as he did at a banquet on February 6, 1934, in San Francisco welcoming Charles

---

34 In fact, Jimmy would live to be seventy-eight, dying on February 16, 1998. He had worked with Herschel at the Coca-Cola bottling plants in Twin Falls and Santa Maria before joining the Lockheed Aviation company and working with that company until he retired.

## HERSCHEL COBB

Two years to the month exactly after the Hankins lawsuit, in December 1932, Herschel Cobb was back in a courtroom in Redwood City, California, on trial for what might be argued was an even tougher charge, this time with his famous father sitting by his side.

Herschel, then eighteen, was accused by a nineteen-year-old female high school friend of assault. She told a jury of two women and ten men that on the evening of February 12, young Cobb invited her to join him and two other young friends, a male and a female, for a ride. She said that she hesitated to go, but her mother said it would be all right.

The Associated Press would quote testimony of the male friend that the foursome drove to a cabin owned by Herschel's father where wine was served. The alleged victim said that she did not drink any. She testified after the other couple left to get some whiskey, Cobb carried her into the bedroom with her struggling. She told the court that she kicked him.

When the other couple returned, the alleged victim said Herschel called her a "cry baby" and offered to take her home. She said, however, first he drove into the hills where he again attacked her until she screamed, and then he drove her home.

The Associated Press story printed in the *Chronicle* on March 20, 1935, quoted a physician as testifying that he examined the girl a few hours after the alleged attack and found "her body bruised, one side of her face swollen and her lips cut."

In spite of the dramatic testimony the *Chronicle*, on March 22, published a one paragraph story headlined, BULLETIN!, with the article saying that "Herschel Cobb, son of the famous former baseball player, Ty Cobb" had been acquitted on the charge of assault and battery.

Herschel apparently lived the next eighteen years without any other serious incidents, working at a Coca-Cola bottling plant in Twin Falls, Idaho, his father had bought. He married and had three children.

On April 13, 1951, he became the first of Ty and Charlie's five children to die, his death from a heart attack coming at the age of thirty-three in Santa Maria, California, where his father owned another Coca-Cola bottling plant.

"Gabby" Street, former St. Louis Cardinals manager, to the San Francisco Mission club in the Coast League. "If I had to do it over again, I wouldn't take baseball so seriously," Cobb said as if anybody really believed him. "In my playing days I was bearing down all the time. I believe I could have cut out a different path than I did.

"There were some mighty fine fellows playing in my days," he continued. "We battled our ways through baseball. It was a fight, tooth and nail. I could have cemented some wonderful friendships in those days with fellows who would be real friends today. I believe I made a mistake there. Baseball is a great game, but there is such as thing as taking it too seriously."

Later that same month in San Francisco, he talked about how much better he liked the climate in California saying, "It is a paradise for the ballplayer when you know what he goes through in the East. I have vivid recollections of those 'cold-one-day' and 'warm-the-next' spring days. Then you run into the hot summers. You rush on trains from one city to another, and the temperature varies from ten to twenty degrees. I was continually troubled with colds and fevers. Since coming to live in California, I have had but one cold and that came right after my arrival."

Cobb still owned the wonderful, two-story Victorian house with its wraparound porch on Williams Street in Augusta. The *Chronicle*, on August 18, 1935, published a small classified advertisement that said, "FOR RENT, 2425 Williams St. Located in one of the best sections of the city. All conveniences. Lockhart, McAuliffe & Co. Phone 640."

The house was still not rented two weeks later and a little larger advertisement using the legend's name appeared in the classified advertising section on September 1, saying, "RENT REDUCED. Ty Cobb Home. 2425 Williams St. 9 Rooms, 2 Baths. Double Garage. Lockhart, McAuliffe & Co., 807 Broad St. Phone 640."

Subsequent ads appeared in early November with the rooms number readjusted and with the rent per month price listed: "FOR RENT—TY COBB HOME, 2425 Williams Street, 8 rooms, 2 baths, double garage. Rent $47.50. Lockhart-McAuliffe & Co. Telephone 640. Masonic Bldg."

Robert Hayes Sherman, who would become vice president of Claussen-Lawrence Construction Company, eventually bought the Williams Street house from Cobb. His father, William Henry Sherman, had been manager of the 1902 team of the Augusta Baseball Association and would be Augusta's representative at the forming of the South Atlantic League in Savannah in November of 1903. Robert H. Sherman would live in the Cobb house until his death on May 10, 1973, and his widow, Alva, continued to live there for several years after that. It was Alva Sherman, in fact, who in the early 1980s graciously allowed this author and another Cobb follower, Richard Corley, to walk through the rooms of the former Cobb home. Before she moved from the house, Mrs. Sherman told this author that she had known the Cobb family growing up and recalled Herschel as being frantic one time over losing one of his father's knives that had four or five blades. "He had to get it back before his daddy found it missing and beat the hell out of him," Mrs. Sherman bluntly said.

Beverly Ford, with her former husband, Terry, bought the Cobb-Sherman house in the spring of 1988 from the Sherman family. There is no historic marker out front, but Cobb fans still find their way to the house. "It seems like once a year, some fans of Mr. Cobb will ride by and stop in," she told the *Chronicle,* noting her son, Billy, had become more of a Ty Cobb historian than she. "They will stay a few minutes and take pictures of the place and usually they will send us some copies of the pictures."

Cobb passed the years of World War II in the early 1940s rather quietly, emerging occasionally in the *Chronicle* and *Herald* headlines as he did on Monday, March 31, 1941, when he made his first visit to the Augusta National course to play golf and see the Masters Tournament. *Herald* sports editor Rut Samuel reported in the afternoon newspaper that Cobb had arrived in town at 2:00 p.m. and was greeted by his host Charley Phinizy and other Augusta friends at Lake Olmstead not far from the course off Washington Road. "Mighty glad to be back," Cobb told his greeters as he warmly shook hands all around. "My, but the old town looks good."

Samuel's account of Cobb's visit subsequently noted, "At three o'clock, the Georgia Peach was teeing off for a round at the Augusta National. He played with Sammy Byrd, former big leaguer who retired to become a golf professional, Charley Yates, former British Amateur champion who lives in Atlanta, Sammy Snead, one of the tourney favorites, and Jerome Franklin of Augusta.

"Cobb hasn't played golf in a month and is just getting over a shoulder injury, sustained when he took a fall while hunting goats, however, he managed to get hold of a few good shots.

"The former Augustan proved that he can come through when the chips are down, as he did in his baseball days, when he holed out a 15-footer to save his side on the ninth. He was on the edge in two, and his putt was 15 feet short. Then needing to save the day for Sammy and Jerome, Cobb got set and knocked it in, the same as he used to come through with base hits with the winning run on base.

"Byrd and Franklin played only nine holes, but Snead, Yates and Cobb finished out the 18. Snead and Yates were in about 75s while Cobb, with three bad holes, had an 87.

"It was Cobb's first visit to the Augusta National, and he was delighted with the course," sports editor Samuel added. "'It's one of the best and most interesting I ever played,' he said. 'It is also very tough to try and figure out. The distances on my second shots fool me. When I think I need a seven or eight iron, I wind up wishing I had used about a four or five.'"

Three months after playing the Augusta National and seeing the Masters Tournament for the first time, Cobb made headlines with three fundraising days of golf luring thousands of spectators. And who was he playing against in the fund-raising matches on June 25, 27, and 29 of 1941: The Great Bambino, Babe Ruth!

In the best two out of three games, Cobb scored 81 to Ruth's 83 on June 25 at the Commonwealth Country Club in Newton, Massachusetts, before

2,000 spectators. Cobb and Ruth both said they were playing "wretched golf," but Cobb's accurate putting won out over Ruth's powerful drives. Cobb said, "This is a very poor round of golf for me." Ruth added, "What else can you do when you keep missing two-footers against a guy who can putt like Ty?"

Only 200 spectators turned out for the second game on June 27 at the Fresh Meadow Country Club on Long Island, New York, with the game being played under a blazing hot sun. The game lasted three hours with the twosome tied at 85 after eighteen holes. Ruth, however, won by one stroke in the playoff nineteenth hole.

## TY COBB AND BABE RUTH

Debate rages to this day about who was the "greatest baseball player of all time." And the top two contenders are usually Ty Cobb and George Herman "Babe" Ruth. Any one who thought there were feelings of ill will between Cobb and Babe Ruth might have had second thoughts in reading that Ruth had picked Cobb as centerfielder on his own "all star baseball array." Ruth had been asked to come up with the list off the top of his head "sitting around the teacups in the locker room after eighteen blustery holes of golf in freezing weather over the course of the North Hempstead country club on Long Island."

Other than Cobb, Ruth listed his ideal team as Hal Chase, first base; Larry Lajoie, second base; Hans Wagner, shortstop; Jimmy Collins, third base; Shoeless Joe Jackson, left field; Harry Hooper, right field; Ray Schalk, catcher; and Christy Mathewson, Eddie Plank, and Herb Pennock, pitchers.

"We've got to give it to Ty because of his offensive ability," Ruth said of picking Cobb as his ideal centerfielder. "He was in a class by himself everywhere but the defense. I would rate Hap Felsch [of the old White Sox] and Tris Speaker far superior on defense."

The third and final game was played on June 29, at the Grosse Ile Golf and Country Club, fifteen miles south of Detroit, which Cobb had played before. Cobb reportedly had labeled the match "The Has Beens Golf Championship of Nowhere in Particular." The temperature was in the nineties but roughly 2,500 fans turned out for the final match. The *Detroit News* would say neither of the legends played their best and that was evident by wild shots hitting six spectators. But, when the last hole was played, the Georgia Peach had beaten the Bambino in one of the most unusual matches the world of golf had ever known.

Cobb's penny-pinching nature was vividly illustrated later in 1941 by a letter he handwrote the great Augusta photographer Frank Christian on September 24, about some photos probably taken during Cobb's March visit to the Augusta National.

Christian's photos of the National and its players would become legendary among worldwide golf fans, and his son, Frank Christian Jr., carried on the tradition as the "official" photographer of the Augusta National and the Masters Tournament.

On September 24, 1941, Cobb wrote the following letter:

> *Mr. Frank J. Christian*
> *Augusta, Ga.*
>
> *Dear Sir:*
> *I have received two statements from you a charge of one dollar each for 12 pictures. I have been away most of the time since your first statement, hence delay in answering.*
> *Shortly after receiving pictures, I wrote acknowledging receipt and, while I did mention a bill, I did not really think I would get one, but if I did I thought it would be far more modest and my statement was more of a polite gesture.*
> *First I want to say, in my many years of baseball and off season and since I retired, I have received thousands or more pictures the boys were good enough to remember me with and not one time have I ever bought*

*one; this goes for [Juan] Montell who you no doubt know [Frank Christian Sr.'s uncle].*

*In Montell's case I have many times put myself out to help him and cooperate. I was informed by him he gained a nice revenue from some of those pictures.*

*In regards to pictures taken of me while in Augusta in April, as far as I was concerned, I was or would be happy to know you benefited by use of me as subject in any way you choosed also it was at your request each time that I posed.*

*[I] Wont you send me a corrected bill under the circumstances or shall I return pictures, as I feel $1.00 each, under conditions I have mentioned, is I think too much.*

*Assuring you of no feelings in the matter, I am,*

*Sincerely,*
*Ty Cobb.*

And then there are letters of a different sort involving Cobb.[35] On March 28, 1942, N. J. L. Pieper, special agent in charge of the San Francisco office, wrote the FBI's director J. Edgar Hoover in Washington, D.C., saying, "Recently Mr. Cobb reported several items of interest and of value to this office in connection with Internal Security and Espionage. . . .

Mr. Cobb specifically mentioned that his friends and he are aware of numerous attempts in the past to discredit the Bureau but that they realize the value of the Bureau to this country's war efforts and have always felt that you, as director of the bureau, and your organization are beyond reproach."

Agent Pieper suggested Hoover might wish to direct a personal letter to Cobb.

Hoover, on April 10, 1942, first wrote Pieper and said, "It is suggested that you may desire to interview Mr. Cobb with the view of developing him as a Special Service Contact." He added, "I believe Mr. Cobb may be

---

35 These letters can be accessed through the Federal Bureau of Investigation's Web site, fbi.gov, using the Freedom of Information Privacy Act link on the home page that offers several letters of public officials and celebrities in the FBI's files.

of invaluable assistance to your office in furnishing information concerning individuals associated with organized baseball."

The same day Hoover wrote Cobb and said, "Mr. N. J. L. Pieper of my San Francisco office has informed me of your whole-hearted cooperation with that office in connection with matters relating to the internal security of this country during this period of emergency. I want you to know that I sincerely appreciate your assistance in this regard and your willingness to continue cooperating with that office.

"I also wish to take this opportunity to personally thank you for your commendatory remarks concerning the work being done by this Bureau and me. I assure you that every attempt will be made by this Bureau to continue operating with the same degree of efficiency in the future."

Pieper wrote Hoover again on June 25, saying that Cobb had been interviewed on June 5 by a special agent from the San Francisco office "at which time Mr. Cobb stated he will give his wholehearted cooperation to the Bureau in any way that the Bureau deems advisable. Mr. Cobb stated that he still maintains close contact with organized baseball and makes trips to the East at irregular intervals during the baseball season to renew old acquaintances and to meet new stars in the baseball world.

"Mr. Cobb advised that he did not believe that there was any subversive element at work among the organized baseball players, and he stated that from his long study and observation that the baseball players and managers as a whole are a loyal and patriotic American group. He stated further that baseball players are very clannish, and that while they talk freely among themselves, the moment an outsider comes in the vicinity they become very secretive and resentful of any outside interference.

"He stated that he could not see how organized baseball as such could be of any value whatsoever to any subversive organization. However, he stated that he would bear the thought in mind henceforward and that in his trips to the eastern part of the United States during the coming season he would be vigilant for any type of subversive activity and would immediately advise the San Francisco Field Division should he detect such."

Several years later, on January 27, 1954, L. B. Nichols [most likely another special agent] wrote Clyde Tolson, aide and very close friend to Hoover.

He reported that Bill Flythe "of the Hearst papers" called and said Cobb was in Washington, D.C., staying in Room 718 of the Mayflower Hotel and "all he wanted to do was to shake hands with the Director while in town."

Mr. Nichols subsequently was informed in an office memorandum dated January 29, that Ty Cobb and his wife [his second wife] visited the FBI's Washington office at 11:00 a.m. on January 28, 1954, and were introduced to Hoover. They had a luncheon engagement they had to attend but returned to the FBI's office at 3:00 p.m. for a special tour that included the exhibit rooms, the FBI laboratory, the Diorama, and the indoor firing range.

As World War II progressed, Cobb's two older sons did not follow their old man overseas in military service, but his oldest daughter did. She already had given up teaching and opened up her first bookstore before the war but decided she wanted to serve with the Red Cross.

"Mr. Cobb didn't want me to buy the bookstore," Shirley Cobb Beckworth recalled, "but I borrowed the money and did it on my own. I worked two years with the Red Cross during World War II in Italy and France, and I was awarded a Medal of Freedom in 1944. I came home, and I had no patience with the American public and their talk of a lack of nylons. I had to leave again and work with the Red Cross in order to keep my bookstore open."

The *Chronicle*, in fact, reported of her service in noting on September 8, 1945, "Shirley Cobb, daughter of the baseball star Ty Cobb, is an American Red Cross clubmobile girl serving with the 85th Division, it has been announced.

"Originally from Augusta, the Cobb family now lives in Menlo Park, California. Shirley managed a bookstore there prior to joining the Red Cross.

"Miss Cobb has served for over a year with the 85th Division serving in Italy and now in Austria. She carries refreshments and entertainment to small groups of soldiers stationed near her area."

It was Shirley, also apparently, who brought the lingering separation of Ty and Charlie Cobb finally to a head. "They were separated for ten years," she told this author, "and I said to my mother, 'For crying out loud, why don't you get a divorce and get all this settled?' She said she wouldn't do anything until I left, so I went to Japan with the Red Cross for two and a half years."

Whether or not that was the real reason Charlie and Ty finally ended their union—officially cemented by their 1908 marriage at The Oaks off Dean's Bridge Road in Augusta—probably never will be known. But in March of 1947, she filed a divorce suit for what would be the final time. Her lawyer was Melvin Belli, who eventually would become world famous for high-profile cases in which he represented Jack Ruby, Zsa Zsa Gabor, Errol Flynn, Chuck Berry, Muhammad Ali, and Sirhan Sirhan, among many others.

On March 14, Belli told reporters he expected Mrs. Cobb to reach an out-of-court settlement in her suit for a division of community property that she set at $7 million and monthly alimony of $5,000. She also asked Cobb to pay $50,000 in attorney fees and $10,000 in court costs. The next day, however, Charlie Cobb withdrew her suit giving no reason for her action. Her attorney, Dan Feeley [possibly a Belli associate or possibly a new attorney] disclosed the withdrawal was preceded by a cash settlement of "around $500,000."

But three months later, in June, it was announced Judge William McKnight in Reno, Nevada, granted a decree of divorce brought by Cobb on the grounds that he and his wife had been separated for at least three years. Cobb, by this time, had established his cabin at Lake Tahoe, Nevada, as his legal residence.

Cobb told reporters in a nutshell, "It was a proposition of convenience."

The Associated Press story of the divorce being granted noted the previous request by Mrs. Cobb for $5,000 monthly alimony and division of the community property which she had set at $7 million. "It was understood the settlement was considerably under half that figure, but that Mrs. Cobb's demands were met," the wire service story said.

Charlie Marion Lombard Cobb would live her final years in a house on Stonegate Road in Portola Valley, California, with her daughter, Shirley, and Shirley's husband, Richard "Dixie" Beckworth. Shirley said her mother had purchased the Stonegate Road house in 1952, "but she couldn't handle the payments by herself. So, Dixie and I moved in with her."

Shirley had met Dixie while serving with the Red Cross in Japan following World War II. They knew each other for five years before getting married and were married for thirteen years until Dixie's death. Shirley said her husband and her father got along great because they both were just country boys. She added, "I'll tell you one thing. Mr. Cobb loved that Dixie Beckworth."

Barely two years after Ty divorced Charlie, he married Frances Cass on September 24, 1949, in Buffalo, New York.

Like Cobb's first marriage forty-one years earlier, it was not a church wedding but a simple ceremony at the home of the bride's father, Dr. John F. Fairbairn, who gave her away. The only witnesses present, as was true of the 1908 marriage, were intimate friends with the officiate being the Reverend William Dudley of Pilgrim First Congregationalist Church.

"It was Cobb's second marriage," the Associated Press reported in a story printed in the *Chronicle* and read by Cobb's old friends back in Augusta. "He was divorced two years ago. Mrs. Cobb has been married twice before. Her first husband [William R. Cass] was killed in an airplane crash 15 years ago. She and her second husband, A. Allen Fusca, were divorced recently. Cobb is 62, his bride is 39."

As for their honeymoon, Cobb said the "only definite plan" was to attend the 1949 World Series. The marriage would last until September 7, 1955, when the second Mrs. Cobb filed for divorce. Six years after that, Tyrus Raymond Cobb would be dead.

THERE IS A SCENE FILMED IN ATHENS, GEORGIA, for the 1994 movie *Cobb* in which the actor who portrays sportswriter Al Stump goes up to a house where Cobb thinks his daughter lives, while Cobb waits in the car. The daughter comes to the door and tells Stump that she doesn't want to see her father. Stump goes back to the car and tells Cobb that they have the wrong house, making for a very touching movie moment.

Unfortunately, it's just not true. It absolutely, positively never happened that way at all.

Cobb always knew exactly where his two daughters and three sons lived and never was turned away. He lived, in fact, right next door to Beverly's house and only five miles from Shirley's.

According to Beverly Cobb McLaren, in his final years, Cobb tried to be a good grandfather to his grandchildren. Beverly had four children, Ty Jr. and Herschel each had three, and Jimmy had five, making fifteen grandchildren. Shirley and her husband didn't have any children.

"If they didn't come home from school when he expected, I'd get a call from him asking, 'Where's Leslie?' [named after Cobb's only sister, Florence Leslie Cobb]. There were fifteen grandchildren; all intelligent and physically well. He thought they were all wonderful."

Cobb wasn't a model grandfather just as he wasn't a model father. But he did try to visit his children and grandchildren now and then. And he did continue to provide generously for them.

Even though he wasn't living in Augusta, Cobb still continued to make the Augusta newspapers whether it was good or bad. On August 24, 1947, the *Chronicle* carried a brief notice that Cobb had been fined $25 in Placerville, California, by a justice of the peace, T. F. Lewis, for drunkenness on public highways. The notice said Cobb didn't appear in court. His attorney, T. S. Marlor, said Cobb "is not well and that concern over the citation had added to his distress." The notice also said Cobb also had been cited the previous month for protesting "volubly after a woman companion was given a traffic ticket."

On October 4, 1947, the *Chronicle* had some very good news to report about Cobb, saying he had made arrangements to donate $100,000 for the construction of a hospital in Royston, Georgia, in memory of his parents, Amanda and Herschel Cobb. It was said the total cost of the hospital would be $250,000 made up of Cobb's gift and federal funds and would serve the northern Georgia counties of Hart, Franklin, Madison, and Elbert. Cobb had been in Los Angeles for the opening of the World Series and then had dropped by Royston to visit his boyhood friend, Dr. Stewart Brown, a northeast Georgia surgeon, the article said.

The next year, Cobb was back in Royston for the groundbreaking of the hospital on March 26, 1949. He would tell reporters, "This is the happiest day of my life. I've never forgotten the people of Royston—my oldest, truest friends." Also present for the groundbreaking was Georgia governor Herman Talmadge, son of the last fiery Georgia governor, Eugene Talmadge, who praised Cobb for his philanthropy in funding the twenty-five-room hospital. Cobb promised he would be back in Royston for the dedication of the hospital, which would come on January 22, 1950.

As Cobb entered the 1950s, he continued to keep up his contacts with the baseball world. He had been inducted into the Baseball Hall of Fame in 1939 in its "freshman" class, but he would not return as an honored guest until June 27, 1953, to witness the induction of other players. Also present at that induction were previous inductees Dizzy Dean, Rogers Hornsby, Connie Mack, Al Simmons, Ed Walsh, and Cy Young.

Cobb skipped the induction ceremony in 1954 but was back in 1955. He skipped 1956 but would be back the next four years: 1957, 1958, 1959. He made his last trip to the Hall on June 27, 1960.

The only other native Georgian inducted into the Baseball Hall of Fame during Cobb's lifetime was Bill Terry of Atlanta. The only other native Georgians inducted after he died (as of this writing) are Jackie Robinson of Cairo in 1962, Josh Gibson of Buena Vista in 1972, and Johnny Mize of Demorest in 1981.

Also, in the 1950s, Cobb became increasingly critical of the changes to the game he loved so much. He was in Atlanta on Tuesday night, August 29, 1950, at Ponce de Leon ballpark, being honored as baseball's greatest when he let loose with some complaints to Don Parker of the International News Service. Parker's article quoted Cobb: "Of what value is the stolen base or the squeeze play now-a-days when it's not uncommon for a team to score 15 or more runs in a single game? In the old days, one run meant something, today a team can build up a ten-run lead, and still lose the ball game in a single inning."

He also told Parker the "new ball" game cheated fans of real baseball.

"How often do you see a modern outfielder cut down a man at the plate who was trying to score from second base? And what has become of the bunt and the hit-and-run?" he added. "In my day, baseball was a close game. The outfielders were part of the team, not just 'caddies' who shagged the long balls."

As Cobb became richer from his Coca-Cola stock, he enjoined his family and friends to invest in the company, always being aware of new developments that would push the stock value even higher. He wrote his friend *Sporting News* publisher Taylor Spink on October 26, 1953, "If you ever buy any stocks, just remember I have written you to buy Coca-Cola now around 108, pays regular $4.00, has always paid and will, always increased their earnings each year and I know now they will show an increase earnings over 1952. Also they have been paying a $1.00 last quarter extra and believe they will this year; that is $5.00 on $108 stock. Also soon a most sensational coin dispenser, not bottles, to be announced. I am buying more now; have advised my daughters also daughter in law, a widow."

The month after writing that letter, Cobb announced another good use of his increasing millions, establishing the Cobb Educational Foundation to help deserving Georgia students get a college or professional education. Cobb joined Dr. Daniel C. Elkin, professor of surgery at Atlanta's Emory University, on November 27, 1953, to announce the fund at a luncheon. Elkin also was announced to be the chairman of the foundation's trustees. Other foundation members included Cobb's second wife, Frances; Dr. Harmon Caldwell, chancellor of the University System of Georgia; and Dr. Fred Rankin of Lexington, Kentucky, a former president of the American College of Surgeons. Cobb said it didn't matter if the earlier education of the Georgia resident applying for the funds had been in the Peach State or not. The fund would be open to girls and boys.

Cobb told the luncheon gathering his father, a schools superintendent, had been disappointed in Ty because he did not go to college. Cobb also said the rural nothern Georgia area produced people of fine character but many lacked formal education. "Out of this reservoir of Lincolnesque people," Cobb said, "if I could get just one boy who'd make something great of himself, I'd feel fully satisfied."

In December of 1954, Cobb was back in Augusta spending two days visiting close friends. He left on December 16, two days before his sixty-eighth birthday.

One year later in December of 1955, Cobb must have felt some of his immortality slipping away with the death, on December 7, of former Pittsburgh Pirate shortstop Honus Wagner at the age of eighty-one. Wagner had been with Cobb in the first group inducted into the Baseball Hall of Fame. "Honus Wagner was the greatest ball player I ever knew," Cobb was quoted as saying upon Wagner's death. "He was a fine competitor and a true gentleman. It was Wagner who helped establish the foundations of baseball. I'm shocked at his death. I'll miss him terribly, and his family has my deepest sympathy."

Cobb may have been shocked at Wagner's death, but he was completely torn up inside two months later with the death of Philadelphia Athletics manager Connie Mack on February 8, 1956, at the age of ninety-three. The Associated Press story said Cobb actually "broke down and cried" when told the news. "I loved Mr. Mack," Cobb said. "You know, a man can love another man. I'm pretty old myself, and I just can't help crying at hearing that he's gone. Everyone loved Mr. Mack. You never heard anyone say anything in criticism of him. Baseball has lost a really great man."

Cobb said the last two seasons of his career, 1927 and 1928, playing for Mack, were the most enjoyable of his time in baseball. "I'd been in the [American] League quite awhile then and I'd been a manager, but when I reported to Mr. Mack I told him I wanted him to wave me to whatever he wanted me to play in the field. He'd do it, and I'd move [to that position], although many times I thought he was making a mistake. But he was always right. He never made a mistake. He was uncanny."

In July of 1957, Cobb was watching a game at the Polo Grounds in New York with sports editor Harry Grayson. He talked about hitting saying, "Left-hand batters should hit left-hand pitches to left field. If the batter closes his stance, he hasn't committed his outside foot, but all they want to do is swing from the end of the bat, and they can't pull against a locked hip. A left-hand pitcher's curve is spinning away from a left-hand batter. He should hit the ball with its strength."

The next month, on August 27, Cobb would be back in Augusta being honored for the third time in his life. Augustans at Warren Park had given him a great send-off when he went to Detroit in 1905, and they publicly had stood up for him at the Confederate Monument in Augusta on a Christmas Eve in the face of the baseball scandal of 1926.

And now on this warm August night in 1957, they would hold "Ty Cobb Night" at Jennings Stadium at Allen Park to honor him once again in his senior years. It was noted Cobb had moved back to northern Georgia after living for many years in California.

More than 3,500 fans not only turned out to see the great Tyrus Raymond Cobb, former Augusta resident, but also to see the Augusta Tigers play the deciding game against the Knoxville (Tennessee) Smokies for the 1957 pennant of the South Atlantic League. The president of the SALLY League, as seen in photos taken with Cobb that night, was Bill Terry, an Atlanta native and former New York Giants player who had been inducted into the Baseball Hall of Fame in 1954.

Johnny Hendrix, sports editor of the *Augusta Chronicle*, wrote about that magical night: "Augusta's Tigers clinched their first South Atlantic League pennant since 1924 last night with a seven-run explosion in the eighth inning that buried Knoxville 9–4. In a drama-jammed situation before more than 3,500 fans who came to pay tribute to baseball immortal Ty Cobb, the Tigers came ripping from behind with an awesome display of bat power to submerge the Smokies, who are trying desperately to clinch a Shaughnessy playoff berth.

"With their hopes of clinching it before the second largest crowd of the season flickering, the Tigers, as they had done so often during the season, came up with more than they needed to insure the victory.

"For Bill Adair, who has bossed this now injury-ridden and recall-riddled outfit, it was his sixth pennant in nine seasons of managing.

"Ty Cobb, the baseball immortal from Royston, Georgia, came back to Augusta last night and in a voice clogged with emotion said thanks to a packed house at Jennings Stadium.

"As John Fetzer, chairman of the board of the Detroit Baseball Co. pointed out, Cobb stood only some two miles from the spot where he got his first hit in professional baseball.

"It was 54 years ago that the 17-year-old Cobb broke into baseball with a home run and a double and one day later found himself released and looking for a job.

"With his mind flooded by memories and his heart filled with feeling for the crowd that turned out, Cobb briefly recalled these early days in what was to become the most fabulous career in baseball.

"When Fetzer presented him with a check for $500—the original price Detroit paid for his contract—the Georgia Peach said, 'I'm flabbergasted.' Then he added, 'It's about time I got that money back, don't you think?'

"But this was only in jest, for it is a recognized fact that Cobb had profited well in a career that spanned 24 years in the big leagues.

"The entire proceeds from the gate of some 3,500 that filled every available seat in Jennings Stadium and ran out into the area around the playing field, went to the Ty Cobb Foundation, along with the check for $500 he received at the introduction from Fetzer.

"'I should feel at home,' Cobb said to the audience, which gave him a standing ovation as he rode onto the field in a convertible from the right field corner. 'But I can assure you that I don't feel much at home in front of this microphone despite the fact that this is home plate and the batters box. I'm just swimming around out here fishing for words. I'm not at ease at all, and I can't tell you how deeply I feel about all this.'

"Earlier in the afternoon, Cobb had confided that the occasion was his first such in a minor league park."

The month after being honored in Augusta, Cobb on September 2, 1957, wrote more about his life back in Georgia to *Sporting News* editor Taylor Spink. Cobb said he owned seventy acres on Chenocetah mountain outside Cornelia, Georgia, covered with rhododendron, dogwood, hemlock, oak, and pine where he could see his grandfather's place "where I was taken to be born some four miles down below my house site" and also could see Toccoa, Georgia, 18 miles away; Lavonia, Georgia, 35 miles; Royston, 35 miles; Athens, Georgia, 45 miles; and Gainesville, Georgia, 26 miles away.

He also planned to have a couple of "real saddle horses" and two "real bird dogs." He noted his land was surrounded by 84,000 acres of government land (Chattahoochee National Forest).

Cobb told Spink that until his house on the mountain could be built, he and his wife were renting a "fine old home here" full of antiques. That home was in Mt. Airy and had been a former Georgia governor's summer residence. He explained why he moved near the place of his birth rather than Royston where he spent his childhood, writing, "I have more relatives around Cornelia than Royston and will be only 40 minutes to Royston."

But his plans to build his mountaintop home fell through as Cobb wrote Spink the next year on November 20, 1958: "Am giving up building a house in Cornelia, Ga. after purchasing 76 acres and a wonderful site, landscaping, drilling a well and all architects plans," he wrote. "Reason, cold as h___ last winter and hot as h___ along with terrific humidity, and no physical outlet, golf, riding or what not."

Cobb also told Spink in the same letter that he had "not been too well though not sick and abed," due to being a prospect for diabetes, not exercising, and having "a fine case of hypertension."

Cobb spent the early part of December 1959 at Emory University

Hospital in Atlanta where he had been undergoing a series of tests and X-rays. He would spend his seventy-third birthday there. Joe Reichler of the Associated Press contacted Cobb at the hospital and was told that Cobb's pet project was to get Hall of Fame recognition for some of the older stars including Eppa Rixey, Sam Rice, Joey Sewell, Edd Roush, Red Faber, and Burleigh Grimes.

Cobb also talked with Reichler about the importance of baseball players staying healthy and in good condition. "I was always aware of the value of being in good condition," he said. "The older I got the harder I worked to get in condition. When you're young, it's easy. You need only five days to get ready. But it's much tougher as you pile on those years. You've got to work longer and harder."

Cobb's medical problems worsened; in his last months his body was racked with pain from cancer, diabetes, severe arthritis, and a chronic heart condition. His thoughts still often turned to his family, and he was not nearly as alienated from them as some writers have suggested.

On March 27, 1961, he wrote by hand in a fairly reasonable script a letter to his only surviving son, Jimmy, and his daughter-in-law, Shirley, in response to being told of the birth of their daughter, Jamie.

> *Dear Shirley and Jimmy:*
> *Telegram was delayed reaching me. You both have been blessed again, and my very good wish to you both and your new child. I realize you might have wanted a boy, but, God, you must remember prevails and is always near. Jim, you can try to get close or closer to him, your way per this. I don't believe [he] has had enough of your attention. My love to mother and child.*
>
> *I am sincerely,*
> *Ty Cobb*

Just a few days later, Cobb sent another short, handwritten note to Jimmy and Shirley's new baby, knowing fully well he would not be around when she grew up.

"Dear Little Miss Cobb," he wrote on April 4, 1961, "I want to be the first of anyone to write you also to say I am happy you arrived safely and hap-

pily and also healthy. It will have to be at some later date, before I will be able
to see you in person, but I will be thinking of you a lot; also loving you.

"Am sure God will protect you in your young life as well as later. I am,
Your Grand Daddy."

Jimmy's wife, Shirley, sent this author copies of those two handwritten letters
with a handwritten note of her own that said, "The dates on the letters should
show that [Al] Stump did depict him quite differently than actual facts. Ty Cobb
died in July 1961. Jamie our youngest died July 3, 1988 (ovarian cancer)."

Years later, Jimmy Cobb in a phone conversation from his home in
California would tell this author of getting a call from his mother in July of
1961. "My mother called one day and said, 'Son, you better go see Daddy.
He's not feeling well.' My sister, Beverly, already was back in Georgia with
our father at Emory University Hospital in Atlanta.

"Beverly told me on the phone, 'You can come, but I can't guarantee you
he'll recognize you. He's in and out.' The next day I got a call from mama
who said, 'I just got a call from Beverly' . . . "

At that point, Jimmy's voiced choked up while talking with this author
and he began to cry softly on the phone.

He continued, saying, "Mama told me that Beverly had told my father
that I had asked about him. He had broken down and cried out, 'I want to
see my boy!' I was on a plane the next day. He knew I was coming, and he
was waiting for me."

Cobb's wife of many years—his sweetheart from his early pro ball playing days in Augusta and the mother of his five children—was there at Emory
hospital in his final hours and would be there at his funeral in Cornelia a few
days later. She spoke privately with him before his death on July 17, 1961,
at the age of seventy-four.

"There was never anyone else in my mother's life," Beverly McLaren
would tell this author. "It was something she wanted to do [be with Cobb at
the end]. Their children were there. It was a united family front.

"I believe, at the end, he recognized that he drove us very hard, and he
was sorry for the unhappiness that had gone on before. . . . He was a very
driven man. He was very ambitious. And he had a difficult time with anyone
not willing to put out their best to excel."

Tyrus Raymond Cobb's body was transported from where he died at Emory University Hospital in Atlanta to McGahee Funeral Home in Cornelia, where he had lived his final years. One of the first to see him before he was put on display in a bronze, glass-topped casket before his funeral was his running buddy, Pope Welborn.

"They brought his body here [to Cornelia], and the local undertaker, Tom McGahee, a friend of mine, held his funeral," Welborn told this author. "They brought him in at night, and I went over there. He was laying out on a morgue table. He didn't have anything on but his shorts. And his legs—they hadn't put him in a suit or anything—where his shorts came to looked like glass. They had been ripped where he had been spiked, I guess. I don't know what else. They were slick, I'm telling you. He would give some and take some, I guess. You could see the scars."

At 3:00 p.m. on Wednesday, July 18, 1961, Cobb's funeral was held in the tiny chapel of McGahee Funeral Home, whose parking lot, ironically, was located where the house once stood where Amanda Chitwood Cobb shot her husband that fateful day in August of 1905. The active pallbearers were Harrison Gailey, the Pontiac dealer and second cousin of Cobb's who caused him to settle in Cornelia his final years, Cliff Kimsey Jr., and Jimmy Freeman, all of Cornelia; Dr. Stewart Brown, for whom he funded the hospital in Royston, and Bob Gree, both of Royston; and Dr. Prentiss Miller and Clark O'Neill, both of Atlanta.

Honorary pallbearers were members of the Cobb Educational Foundation and the staff of Cobb Memorial Hospital.

Years later, detractors of Cobb would point to the lack of many major-league ballplayers at his funeral, not mentioning it was held at the height of baseball season when players were in heated games nor considering Cobb had been away from professional baseball for more than thirty years!

Still, attendees at his funeral did include baseball greats Mickey Cochrane, formerly of the Philadelphia Athletics and Detroit Tigers; Ray Schalk, formerly of the Chicago White Sox; Nap Rucker, Cobb's playing partner on the old Augusta Tourists and himself a professional ballplayer; and Sid Keener, director of the Baseball Hall of Fame in Cooperstown.

And also in the tiny chapel were his daughters, Beverly McLaren and Shirley Beckworth; his son, Jimmy; his former wife, Charlie; and several of Cobb's fifteen grandchildren. It was said Cobb's only brother, John Paul Cobb, then seventy-two, could not attend due to suffering a paralytic stroke several years earlier.

The services were conducted by the Reverend E. A. Miller, pastor of the Cornelia Christian Church, and the Reverend Dr. John R. Richardson, pastor of Westminister Presbyterian Church in Atlanta. Miller would say, "In his field of endeavor, he won just about everything that could be won. His influence will continue to bring the best out of youth. Ty Cobb was never satisfied with second best."

Man, wasn't that the truth!

Following the funeral, the body was carried in a procession twenty-eight miles away to the white mausoleum in Royston where the bodies of his mother, father, and sister already were entombed. There were about 200 Little League ballplayers lined up from the cemetery entrance to the mausoleum where the greatest ballplayer in the world would have his final resting place.

Just as his name had been mentioned so prominently in the Augusta newspapers all of his life, so it was that he was prominently mentioned in them at the time of his death.

The *Augusta Herald* wrote in an editorial on July 18, 1961, "Since the story of Ty Cobb is so closely interwoven with that of Augusta's sports history, the great baseball player's death yesterday at age 74 was, while not unexpected, nonetheless a shock to many local citizens who remembered him as one of them and who for a quarter-century followed his incandescent athletic career."

The *Herald* noted the good and bad points of the Augusta legendary figure and concluded, "Such impetuous outbursts were a part of the man, and without them it is likely he would have lacked the 'steam' and color and courage that were to make him the greatest baseball player of all time. It should here be noted, however, that it was generally said of him that he never forgot a friend.

"At any rate, Tyrus Raymond Cobb, the 'Georgia Peach,' will be a legend as long as baseball is a part of the American scene."

And one of the finest tributes of all was by Johnny Hendrix, the sports columnist for the *Augusta Chronicle*, who recalled being with Cobb the last time he was honored in Augusta four years earlier in 1957.

"It was different in the dugout that night," Hendrix recalled. "Most of the players were there much earlier than usual after batting practice and infield. They stood in the runway that led from the dressing room, leaned on the bat rack or sat on the bench. Some of them stood in front looking up into the crowd that was buzzing with a sense of expectation.

"When he came in and started shaking hands, everybody else stopped talking for awhile. He was a big man in a brown suit that could have used a press job and his necktie had one of those knots that was outdated by the Duke of Windsor.

"'He don't look like no millionaire to me,' somebody said almost in a whisper. 'He don't look like he coulda hit no three hundred and something for 24 years in the big leagues, neither. He looks like some farmer come to town on Saturday.'

"This was the night Augusta clinched its first pennant in 33 years in the South Atlantic League, but the some 3,500 people in the stands weren't there primarily for that. The Tigers, leading the league by 16 games, had long been conceded that plum. The people in the stands, from eight-or-less to eighty-or-more had come to take a look at Tyrus Raymond Cobb, a living baseball legend, the first man to be elected to the Hall of Fame and holder of a few dozen other major accomplishments.

"To the ballplayers, most of all of whom were born after Cobb had quit the game, he was a man they had heard of all their lives. To the people in the stands, the same held true for a good portion and for some, there was the sweetness of the memories of having seen him before he clawed his way to recognition as the greatest player who had ever lived.

"It was hard—no impossible—to see him as the figure in the newspaper clippings of old and of the books and stories that had been written about him.

"This man in the brown suit, the glasses without rims and the out-of-style knot in his necktie could not be that dare-devil of the basepaths, magician with the bat, the smartest head a player ever carried and the inferno of desire that at one time owned some 90 individual major league playing records.

"His reputation for meanness was dissipated completely when he stood in front of the grandstand, tears in his eyes and in halting, but firm voice said his appreciation for the honor of having a night dedicated to him in the town where he got his start.

"So this was Ty Cobb on his last visit to Augusta. He enjoyed it a great deal, he said. It was the first time he had even been honored in a minor league park, one of the few things remaining which might have added to the pleasures of his waning years.

"Later that night, he came to the door of his room at the Bon Air Hotel. He didn't have on the coat to the suit any more and he had pulled the tie loose from his neck. It hung to one side, giving the impression that he was a little out of balance.

"'Why don't you come up and visit me later tonight,' he had asked in the afternoon when the suite was crowded and he was being taken down memory lane with Bill Terry.

"Now he said in a fashion that was full of sincerity, 'I'm glad you were able to come.'

"So, we sat and talked into the wee hours of the morning, nothing between us but a bottle of whiskey and a lifetime of experiences, experiences that could fill a best seller.

"'You asked about the place I'm going to build at Royston,' he said. 'It's something I always wanted to do. I like to talk about it. I don't get to visit with people who like to hear an old man talk about the place he wants to build to go and die.'

"He never built that place. I don't know why, exactly. But I can still hear him describing it and the view from the top of the mountain. I don't think I'll ever forget it."

# EPILOGUE: THE COBB LEGACY

IT'S A WEDNESDAY AFTERNOON on September 1, 1982, and this author is on the telephone in Augusta, Georgia, talking with Shirley Cobb Beckworth, oldest daughter of the legendary Ty Cobb at her bookstore in Palo Alto, California. She says with complete candor: "At the end, he had millions but he had nothing. His was a wasted life, and he died a lonely, lonely man. But every man's opinion of what life should be is different.

"It was too bad Mr. Cobb didn't go into medicine like his father wanted. He shouldn't have retired at forty-one. A man with that much energy shouldn't retire at that age. I remember going to his house and seeing him sitting in a chair inside. It was when I could finally talk back to him. I said, 'Are you going to dig a hole like a dog and crawl into it? It's a beautiful day. Get out and do something.'"

Before we hung up she said to me, "You be careful of what you print. I'm a good shot."

Shirley and her sister, Beverly, and her brother, Jimmy, whom I had talked with in my early days of Cobb research, no longer are alive, and yet I still have felt their presence throughout the course of the writing of this book.

Do I want them to approve of everything I've written? Of course not. Do I want them to think I have tried to be more than fair and exceptionally accurate in the depiction of their father and mother? Without a doubt, yes.

Within a few months after Cobb's death in 1961, sports fans were offered Al Stump's highly inaccurate ghost-written book, *My Life in Baseball: The True Record.* Stump would make another attempt at documenting the baseball legend in the 1994 book, *Cobb: A Biography.*

The view of Cobb's family, friends, and close supporters of Stump's work is pretty much the same as that expressed by his oldest daughter, Shirley Cobb Beckworth, in a conversation with this author on September 1, 1982. She said, "Al Stump is the biggest louse I know. Mr. Cobb wanted Gene Fowler to write his book. I figured if he [Fowler] could take [actor] John Barrymore and make him lovable, he could do it for Mr. Cobb. But Mr. Fowler was dying of cancer, and he didn't have much time. Mr. Cobb showed me some pages Al Stump had written, and I told him, 'Look at these slang words. I never heard you use slang in your life.' It wasn't Ty Cobb."

His other daughter, Beverly Cobb McLaren, would tell me, "Al Stump was with him in his later years at a very lonely time. He was alienated from his family then. He was very difficult. He was a lonely, unhappy man in his last years."

Cobb's youngest son, Jimmy, at the age of seventy-three, would say of Stump in 1995, "I've never met the man, but this thing was like a vendetta. I mean, how would you like to have someone say things like that about your father? It's very upsetting. We've tried to control some of this, but it's hard to. This has hurt the family very much. . . . One night I just sat down and cried. I thought about all the bad things people were saying and writing, and I just let it all out, and I felt better. I know what he did, and he did a lot of good things."

Cobb's will, signed "Tyrus R. Cobb" on May 22, 1961, attested to those good things. He left 25 percent of his estate to the educational fund he had established eight years earlier for needy students and the remaining 75 percent in trust for his children and grandchildren. Assuming the reports of his net worth of $7 to $8 million are true, then that means Cobb willed about $2 million to the educational foundation.

Shirley Cobb Beckworth was authorized by name in the will to dispose of Cobb's personal effects with the will stating, "All of my personal effects,

EPILOGUE: THE COBB LEGACY

including awards, trophies, mementoes, clothing, jewelry, household furniture and furnishings, books, pictures, silverware, automobiles and other such personal effects, shall be distributed to such persons and in such manner as my daughter, SHIRLEY COBB BECKWORTH, shall direct. I expect to leave a letter giving directions as to certain items, and I know she will follow my directions. As to items in regard to which I do not give directions, she shall be authorized to turn over such of my awards, trophies, and mementoes so such museum or museums as she may deem most suitable, and the remaining items she shall distribute among such of my descendants as she shall deem best."

Cobb Memorial Hospital in Royston already had been dedicated on January 22, 1950, funded with a $100,000 gift from Cobb to preserve the memories of his mother and father. The hospital would evolve into the Ty Cobb Healthcare System. It still is billed as "The Hospital Built with a Bat" and "Home Base for Good Health."

## THE HEALTHCARE SYSTEM NOW CONSISTS OF THE FOLLOWING:

♦ *Cobb Memorial Hospital,* Royston, Georgia, a 71-bed, medical and surgical hospital

♦ *Hart County Hospital,* Hartwell, Georgia, a 98-bed medical and surgical hospital

♦ *Brown Memorial Convalescent Center,* Royston, a 144-bed hospital-based long-term care facility located adjacent to Cobb Memorial Hospital

♦ *Cobb Health Care Center,* Comer, Georgia, a 116-bed hospital-based long-term care facility

♦ *Hartwell Health Care Center,* Hartwell, Georgia, a 92-bed hospital-based long-term care facility

♦ *Home Base Health Services,* Royston and Hartwell, a home medical equipment service that provides IV home infusion services and home medical equipment, including respiratory home care, beds, wheelchairs, apnea monitor services and sleep disorder services

- *Cobb Terrace Personal Care Center,* Royston, an 18-bed hospital-based personal care home that provides a positive alternative to living alone
- *Cobb Center Inc.,* Royston, a 24-unit HUD independent living housing complex (eighteen one-bedroom and six efficiencies) for persons sixty-two and older, managed by the Ty Cobb Healthcare System, with the rental prices based on limited income
- *Healthworks, Hartwell* and *Royston,* occupational health and wellness services that consist of on-site drug screen collection and breath alcohol testing, OSHA safety training classes, HealthShare and comprehensive corporate wellness programs, which include computerized health and fitness assessments
- *Wee Care Rehab,* Royston, a complete team of pediatric therapists, pediatric speech therapists, and pediatric occupational therapists who provide outpatient rehabilitation to help children achieve maximum independence
- Physician Practices, consisting of *Hart County Medical Associates,* an internal medicine medical practice in Hartwell; *Franklin County Medical Associates,* a primary care medical practice in Carnesville, Georgia; and *Women's Health Specialists of North Georgia* offering obstetrics and gynecology services in Royston and Lavonia, Georgia
- *Ty Cobb Kidney Care,* Royston, a 13-station, state-of-the-art dialysis center
- *Cobb Terrace Assisted Living Center,* Royston, a 48-bed assisted-living facility

There is also the Ty Cobb Museum, a not-for-profit institution in Royston that "fosters an appreciation for the life and career of Tyrus Raymond Cobb, provides information about baseball history during Cobb's era, and his impact on the game of baseball." While focusing on the baseball accomplishments of Ty Cobb through exhibits, film presentation and artifacts, the museum also focuses on other positive accomplishments in the areas of education and health care.

Since July of 1998, the museum, in the Joe A. Adams Professional Building, 461 Cook Street, has attracted thousands of visitors from throughout the world. It is open 9:00 a.m. to 4:00 p.m. Monday through Friday and 10:00 a.m. to 4:00 p.m. Saturday, closed on some holidays, with admission being $5 for adults, $4 for persons sixty-two and older, $3 for students, and free to military persons and children four and younger. (Visit the Web site tycobbmuseum.org for other details.)

Three years after his death, the Georgia Athletic Hall of Fame was created and Cobb was inducted as one of three charter members, along with golfer Bobby Jones and Georgia Tech's long-time football coach Bill Alexander. Accepting Cobb's plaque on February 15, 1964, in Atlanta were his daughter, Shirley, of Palo Alto, California, and his grandson, Charlie Cobb (son of Ty Jr.) of Daytona Beach, Florida.

Addressing the audience Georgia's Governor, Carl E. Sanders, a native of Augusta who grew up with the legend of Cobb, remarked, "There is doubt that any state in the union can boast of such sports Gargantuans as we have chosen for our initial Hall of Fame induction tonight.

"Look at the list: Bobby Jones, the world's first and only undisputed golf champion; Ty Cobb, voted in every poll the greatest ballplayer who ever lived; and Bill Alexander, who firmly established Georgia Tech as a national football power, a position she so preeminently still occupies."

Former golf player Cobb probably would have loved the first Ty Cobb Memorial Golf Tournament held July 16, 1999, at the Cateechee Golf Club in Hartwell, Georgia, "to benefit Ty Cobb Healthcare System and The Ty Cobb Museum." The entry fee was $60 per player, which included lunch, door prizes, and eighteen holes of golf with a cart supplied.

As noted earlier, one of the greatest things Cobb did other than funding the Royston hospital and its subsequent health-care offerings was establishing the Cobb Educational Foundation in 1953 to help deserving Georgia students get a college or professional education and leaving in his will 25 percent of his estate to the educational fund in 1961.

On February 4, 2004, reporter Preston Sparks noted in the *Augusta Chronicle* that two months earlier the office for administering the educational scholarship had moved to Augusta, appropriately enough, since it was where Cobb once played professionally and lived. Francis Tedesco, a member of the foundation's board and a former Medical College of Georgia president, apparently was instrumental in having the office moved from Forest Park, Georgia, near Atlanta, to an office in Augusta provided by the Medical College of Georgia.

Tedesco told Sparks that the location was ideal not only because of Cobb's connection to Augusta, but also because the foundation has provided thousands of scholarship dollars to MCG students. "I thought it was a natural," Dr. Tedesco said. "He had a great love for education and supporting Georgians."

Sparks also noted that Cheryl O'Keeffe, director of student financial aid at the Medical College of Georgia, had become the foundation's new secretary in Augusta.

According to the Web site tycobbfoundation.com, there have been more than 7,251 scholarships totaling more than $10,637,123 awarded from the foundation. Let me rephrase that: **The Georgian who many writers and critics say was one of the most hated persons who ever lived now has provided a means for more than 7,200 students to achieve higher education and better their lives, having generously provided more than $10.6 million in scholarship money!**

My guess is you will not find too many of those 7,251 scholarship recipients saying anything bad about Cobb.

The foundation Web site also states the requirements for those applying for the scholarships:

"Undergraduate students who are residents of Georgia, have demonstrated financial need, and have completed at least 30 semester or 45 quarter hours of academic credits with an average of 'B' or higher in an accredited college or university are eligible to apply for Ty Cobb scholarships.

"Students with higher academic averages and the greatest financial need will be given priority.

"Professional students in medicine and dentistry who are residents of the State of Georgia and have demonstrated financial need are eligible to apply for Ty Cobb scholarships."

In 2003, Georgia state senator Carol Jackson of the fiftieth district, which includes eight northern Georgia counties surrounding Cobb's birthplace, sponsored Senate Resolution 798 "recognizing the 50th anniversary of the Ty Cobb Educational Foundation." The resolution noted the foundation had provided more than $10 million in scholarships to resident area students and "the initial investment by Cobb was the donation of 250 shares of Coca-Cola stock to a fund at the Trust Company of Georgia, now SunTrust Bank, the funds' permanent trustee institution."

Additionally, the resolution proposed the members of the Georgia Senate "commend the Ty Cobb Educational Foundation for its generous contributions to aspiring students all across this state."

At this writing, Cobb's former hometown of Augusta has been reluctant in honoring the world's greatest baseball player or capitalizing on the fame of the former, longtime resident. The only thing bearing his name is the Cobb House apartments at 10th and Greene Streets that he built and originally named after his daughter, Shirley.

There is no historic marker at the Exchange Club of Augusta fairgrounds where Cobb first started playing professional ball in 1904 and where he would bring the Detroit Tigers to play exhibition games against other major-league teams.

There is no historic marker in front of his former home on Williams Street near Augusta State College, none at Seventh and Broad Streets where he had his tire store, and none at the Augusta Country Club where he played golf.

With the addition of the James Brown statue, there were seventeen life-size statues in the city of Augusta of which six are of golfers, including Bobby Jones and Jack Nicklaus; five of Confederate soldiers; and there is one each of a British general, a Confederate poet, a former U.S. senator, a Presbyterian minister, and Miss Justice with her scales.

But there is no statue of Ty Cobb, no tourism brochure showing local places associated with him, and no street named after him.

Bill Kirby, metro editor and popular columnist of the *Augusta Chronicle* on December 21, 1994, urged tolerance and understanding of Cobb, writing, "So, when remembering Ty Cobb, born five score and eight years ago Dec. 18, let's separate the player from the person. He completed a stellar baseball career with the highest batting average ever. His contemporaries considered him the best to play the game, better even than Babe Ruth.

"He was a shrewd businessman who made several fortunes outside of sports. And before he died, he built and endowed a hospital in his hometown of Royston and dedicated it to his parents.

"History doesn't usually remember folks for being kind and generous. It remembers them for what they accomplished. And Ty Cobb is recalled as being the best all around ballplayer in history."

Over the years, many who have championed Cobb have recommended the best tribute would be to rename the city of Augusta's 4,400-seat baseball stadium—now bearing the boring name Lake Olmstead Stadium—where the Augusta Greenjackets minor league team plays to large crowds, after Cobb.

There is hope the Greenjackets new owner, baseball legend Cal Ripken Jr., will remedy that oversight with a plaque or a marker or anything else, even though he does not have the authority to rename the stadium after Cobb.

Cobb fan Dave Goodbread of Augusta also championed the cause when the Lake Olmstead Stadium was being constructed. He wrote in a letter to the editor of the *Chronicle* in October of 1994, "Baseball is a game that draws its strength from its own heritage. In Augusta, we have the unique advantage of claiming a baseball immortal as our own.

"I propose we honor Ty Cobb's significance to baseball by naming the playing field at the new stadium 'Ty Cobb Field,'" Goodbread added. "If the members of the stadium committee wish to dedicate the entire facility to him, that is fine, but I do think that, at a minimum, the playing field should bear his name."

Goodbread concluded, "Dedication of the new field in Cobb's honor will be an excellent tribute to both his sporting accomplishments and his ties to this community."

Unfortunately, that suggestion also fell on deaf ears.

In the meantime, many places associated with Cobb still exist, although Warren Park where he played and Allen Park where he was honored in 1957 are around no more and the grandstand at Warren Park and the Jennings Stadium at Allen Park have long since been demolished.

There are grandchildren and distant cousins of Cobb's now scattered throughout the United States, but the closest relatives of his children and nieces and nephews have died off. The last nephew or niece on his wife's side of the family was Dr. Elna Anne Lombard, who died April 29, 2006, at the age of eighty-eight at her home where The Oaks once existed; that being the former home of Elna's grandparents where Ty Cobb married Charlie Lombard in 1908.

Dr. Lombard, daughter of Cobb's son, Roswell Harmond Lombard, and his wife, Anne Schmidt Lombard, was trained as a musician and professional dancer before becoming one of the first Women's Army Corps volunteers from the Augusta area in World War II, making the rank of captain in 1944.

She studied at the Medical College of Georgia, as did Ty Cobb Jr., with her specialty being psychiatry. She became director of the Mental Health Center in Aiken, South Carolina, and later director of the Mental Health Association in Augusta. She also became a pilot, an excellent golfer like her famous uncle, and a state bowling champion.

When she died, she left her historic home site and other property to her close friend of forty-seven years, Margaret Holley. Elna, like her uncle, was a baseball fan, and she and Margaret were preparing once again to buy season tickets for the Augusta Greenjackets when she died.

Just across Old U.S. Highway 1 from the family house is the old Lombard Mill Pond site that now is a fifty-acre parcel of publicly conserved green space. It is part of the Butler Creek Nature Corridor being developed by the American Hiking Society's Volunteer Vacation program. The volunteers have been working on a 1.5-mile loop trail around the Lombard Mill Pond complete with wooden boardwalks and bridges. (Visit the Web site csrlt.org to know more about this project.)

Unless there is some marker erected, those walking beside the pond will never know the land formerly belonged to the father-in-law and mother-in-law of Ty Cobb and that the world's greatest baseball player began his family life with a simple marriage ceremony just across the road from the property.

Maybe the ultimate honor for Cobb in his former hometown of Augusta would be to name for him the walking trail around the pond that he himself surely must have once walked around during his stays and visits to the Lombard home.

For there is a quiet and peacefulness in those deep woods around the Lombard pond like which Tyrus Raymond Cobb must have experienced hunting in the woods of Georgia and South Carolina or golfing on local courses far away from the noisy crowds at the baseball diamonds that brought him worldwide fame and immortality, and far away from his occasional detractors.

And there is no doubt that being with his friends and family at such places during the quarter century that he lived in Augusta is what made Ty Cobb feel truly safe at home.

# Appendix: An Interview with Pope Welborn

ONE OF THE MOST INSIGHTFUL CONVERSATIONS this author had about Cobb's final years came on August 15, 1982, in Cornelia, Georgia, in talking with Pope Welborn, who claimed to be one of Cobb's closest friends during those final years.

Welborn took this author and another Cobb enthusiast, Richard Corley, to the rural area where Cobb was born, the small brick apartment in Cornelia where he spent his final days, and other local sites associated with Cobb.

Even if Welborn was making any of his comments up, he still had a remarkable knowledge of Cobb, and most of what he said that day has been confirmed by Cobb's daughters and other sources.

So, here are the remarkable tales Pope Welborn told us that warm August day. You can decide for yourself what to believe.

AUTHOR: How long have you been living in Cornelia?

WELBORN: Right to the day? Since November 6, 1908, . . . seventy-four years.

AUTHOR: That's the year he married his wife, Charlie.

WELBORN: Is that right?

AUTHOR: When Ty moved here, were you aware who he was?

WELBORN: Oh, yeah. You have a feeling about somebody you've read about and heard about all of your life, and that's the way it was when I was a kid in the twenties during and after World War I. I was ten years old when World War I was over [1919]. It gave you sort of a shaky feeling to meet someone like that, notable as he was.

I had a tire recap shop [in Cornelia] called Welborn's Gulf Station, and he was a customer. I had a service department too—washing, greasing, and all that. This was about 1958, 1959, and 1960.

AUTHOR: Do you know that Ty Cobb also was in the tire business in the 1920s?

WELBORN: 1920! You wouldn't think there'd be enough cars then to sell tires. . . . Ty has a second cousin here, William Harrison Gailey, who had a Pontiac dealership next to my station. He was in a terrible automobile wreck, and he has heart trouble too. That's one reason Ty came back here. He bought some acreage on the mountain, about sixty-five acres, and he was going to build a house up there. Chenocetah Mountain. Ty would use his cousin's secretary to write letters [such as the one to *Sporting News* editor Frank Spink]. Really that was how come for me to be so close to him. He would come down there to see his cousin and get the secretary to write letters for him, and I met him there.

I had a cabin up on Lake Burton, a Georgia Power Company lake on the headwaters of the Savannah River, and we'd go up there every Wednesday. I would close on Wednesday afternoon, and we'd go up there and cook some steaks and take a bottle. We'd make a side trip every Wednesday afternoon for I guess two years.

There wasn't a bottle store here then, and it's about twenty miles to the South Carolina line to the Tugalo River, which is the headwaters of the Savannah [River], and we'd go to this bottle shop. He had a flask holder. It would hold five fifths. It was in a circle. He carried that thing with him all the time. That's a gallon. He wouldn't drink anything with it but Coca-Cola, 'cause he had a lot of Coca-Cola stock. About $7.5 million worth, his banker and my banker told me. But anyway we'd go over to a liquor store in South Carolina where it was legal to buy legal booze. Then we would take a back cut out of South Carolina over to Clayton, Georgia, and then over to my cabin on Burton Lake, and we'd stop on the way to buy steak, fish, or whatever we'd want to eat. We'd stay until about midnight and then come home. He'd drink bourbon just about all together.

Every time he'd go, he would buy two bottles of bourbon, Jack Daniels. He would put the two bottles in the carrying case, and he had one in the center. He had Coca-Cola in that. Then, what he would do before he'd leave when he got a bottle empty, he would put two or three ounces of bourbon in it, then fill it up with Coca-Cola. It would look like bourbon. Then when he wanted to take a drink, he already had his chaser and all mixed. Everybody was thinking he was drinking pure liquor.

He could drink all day, but he was drinking Coca-Cola really. It was just spiked a little. We carried on like that in '58, '59, and '60. Then in the fall of '60, my wife died of cancer. Cobb had gone back to California. He'd been out there about a month, and he got the little local paper here, and he saw where my wife had died. So he called me and he told me there was a ticket in Atlanta, just pick it up and get on the plane. I stayed out there about a month I guess.

My wife died October 6, and I already had planned to go on a deer hunt. We'd been going, a bunch of us, fifteen to twenty years. Well, I told Ty I would go on the deer hunt and then leave on the Saturday after Thanksgiving, and I did. Then you couldn't fly directly from Atlanta to San Francisco. You had to fly to Los Angeles and change to Trans World, but that's another story all together.

He told me to call him when I got to L.A. and to give him my flight number since I might miss my connection out of there. I didn't have time, but I gave the number to an information booth and had them call him, and he met me at the airport with his son-in-law, Dixie Beckworth, and his daughter, Shirley. Ty and his [second] wife had separated then.

I never will forget, we went to a restaurant that was supposed to close at midnight. He had called the restaurant and asked them to stay open. The name of it was The Willows. It had a bar, of course, and we had a bottle of wine for the four of us. He was driving a little old Thunderbird that belonged to Dixie. I know that thing sure was full with big old long-legged Ty in it.

Ty had come to Georgia and lived here a year and thought he would move his residence here, but he got in a squabble with the government, and it cost him about $150,000 in Georgia and California income taxes. He had moved to Georgia, but he didn't cut his California utilities off. They checked, though, and found out he wasn't a bona fide resident of Georgia, so then he cut everything off in California.

His daughter, Beverly, lived next door, and he had a long wire drop cord for electricity. He didn't have a refrigerator or a stove. He just had one light, and he carried it around in this big Spanish-type house that looked like a fort. It had two stories on the front, and then a backside and that side and that side. There was a closed in court in the back with a big orange tree in the middle of it. There wasn't any lights, and we couldn't stay there at night, but he had a lot of logs left over from this fireplace. This was in early November but it never gets that cold in San Francisco. We'd build a big fire in late afternoon and stay there until dark or a little later. Then we'd go somewhere and eat, and then go stay in a motel.

(At this point, Welborn showed Corley and this author a green Algiers Motel towel.)

We went down El Camino Real, that's the Kings Way, to the Algiers Motel. I got this towel from there one morning to clean the car windshield. The motel was just south of San Francisco. I believe it was almost directly between the Cow Palace and Candlestick Park. It was right close. When he would check in anywhere, he would just sign, 'Mr. Cobb.'

He wouldn't let me get another room. He'd get double beds, and I would stay in the room with him. That motel had a bowling alley and a restaurant next to it. I'd get up in the morning, and I'd go to the restaurant and have them break two eggs in a big glass and put a spoonful of sugar in it and then fill it up with milk. He would drink about an ounce of it out, and that's all he'd have for breakfast. He wouldn't have that until about ten o'clock. Then he'd fill it up with bourbon and shake the raw eggs up in there.

CORLEY: Was he a big eater later in the day?

WELBORN: At night, yeah, until midnight. He would be up until six thirty or seven o'clock. If he didn't go to bed, he would start another day. Boy, he was an iron horse. I'm telling you.

There was this Chinese place he would want to go there every night, and he'd want to go late. I mean, nine, ten, or eleven o'clock. We went to this Chinese restaurant, and I drove the car, a big old Chrysler Imperial, into the yard. He didn't like where I parked it. He was, of course, still drinking. He said, "Oh, hell, you can't drive! Let me back it up!" And he backed it into a late forties Plymouth and hung up the two bumpers.

They couldn't find the guy who owned the car. The cafe security guard came out there and, of course, they didn't make a case against him. The guard did ask him for his driver's license, and, of course, he gave it to them. When the guard said, 'Ty Cobb,' everybody around there came up. They all got a hold of the car and picked his car up and got the cars apart. He gave the security guard his number at the motel [where] we were staying and told him to call him the next morning and he would talk to him, and he did, and he gave him his insurance.

We went on in the restaurant, and, of course, there was bamboo and Chinese lanterns all around. He went in the door hollering, "Charlie!" This little Chinaman came up and said, "Yes, sir, could I please help you, please?" He was just a bowing and bending and Ty said, "I want to see Charlie." The Chinaman said, "Charlie, he a very busy man. You no see Charlie tonight." Ty said, "By God, I'll see Charlie tonight!" He was yelling, "Charlie!" The restaurant was crowded. The Chinaman took off and he came out with Charlie, who apparently was the owner. Of course, when he was told how Ty was acting, he knew it was Ty. He said, "Yes, sir, Mr. Cobb. Sorry me late. Got here as quick as I could."

Ty ordered just about everything in the place. Some things I didn't know what they were. That same Chinaman who first met us also waited on our table, and Ty tipped him a twenty-dollar bill. Ty didn't apologize to anybody.

AUTHOR: It wasn't his style to apologize to anybody, was it?

WELBORN: Nooo. He'd insult you before he did that. He was generous with his tips, everywhere and at all times, and yet he could be tight with his money. One time when we went to a beer joint just across the line in South Carolina, he said, "I feel like driving." When he got out of the car—he was a big guy anyway—a penny slid out of his pocket and went somewhere. He got out, and got down on his knees, and looked under the seat. I said, "Ty, let's go. It's just a penny." He said, "Well, hell, a penny's money!" . . . I knew the president of his bank here, and we had heard and read in the paper that

Ty was worth $10 million, but Cliff told me it was $7.5 million. He said, "I had it audited and checked it out."

AUTHOR: It seems like he was a generous person at some times.

WELBORN: Until he started drinking.

AUTHOR: Was he like a Dr. Jekyl and Mr. Hyde personality?

WELBORN: Absolutely. Absolutely. He told me, "I never drank a drop of anything until I retired from baseball," and I was surprised at that. You know he would take an occasional drink. I sort of felt that and could read between the lines. What he meant was he wouldn't drink all the time when he was off at night.

He'd insult you right quick. He got so mad at me one night, and I got mad enough to kick him. He was living in this house in Mount Airy [next to Cornelia], and he called me up. He said, "I'm running low. Let's go to South Carolina." But it wasn't a Wednesday, and I was open. I said, "The boy that works here needs to take his wife to the hospital, and I can't go." He said, "What time is he going to leave?" and I said, "He'll leave at six o'clock," and he said, "I'll have you back by six."

So he came for me, and we got over there to South Carolina, and, of course, he opened a bottle up, and we started back. He said, "Let's go stop at my house and have another drink." I said, "I've got to go at six o'clock." He said, "Oh, hell, come and go with me. I'm looking out after you." So we went in, and he had one, and then he had another, and it got to be six o'clock. I didn't know he had a telephone. He had an unlisted telephone, but he didn't say anything to me about it, and I didn't ask him. So, I couldn't call the boy and tell him to lock the door and go on to the hospital.

I got mad and started out the door, and Ty got yelling at me. I got two or three hundred yards on the highway. He cranked his car up and came up beside me on the highway, but I wouldn't get in. He was driving along the road, and I was walking along the side and calling him everything I could think of. So I finally got in, and he brought me down to the station but the boy already had gone.

So the next morning I said to myself, "Well, I guess that's the last of Ty Cobb." But about seven o'clock about the time I opened up, here he comes all dressed up, cleaned up spic and span. I was the only one at the station, so I got out and walked out there, and I threw up my hand and I said, "Hi." I'll tell you the exact words he said, but I don't think you can put it down. He said, "Goddamn! That's the way I like to see 'em bounce back!" So put something else in there.

It wasn't too long after that when my wife died, and I went out there [to California.] He was going to ride back to Georgia with me driving his car, but he was too sick, so I drove his car and he flew back. He was still trying to save on that income tax he had to pay to the state of California and was moving back to Georgia. So, I brought his car back and his personal belongings—what we could get in his Chrysler Imperial. It was an old one. It was scratched up like a dog had slept in it. That's right. He did trade it for a Pontiac not long before he passed away. I brought back his shotguns and most of his clothing. Then he flew back here and moved out of the big house in Mount Airy and took an apartment in Cornelia.

Al Stump for *True Magazine* wrote an article about Ty, and a lot of it wasn't true. He didn't have that [German Luger pistol] the three or four years that I knew him, and every time we stayed anywhere, I stayed in the room and would have seen it. The part about him having a gun [pistol] and shooting through the door at Carson City sounded like a bunch of malarky. Ty didn't even have a gun except for some old, expensive shotguns, as far as I knew, and I drove back from California all his securities. They were registered to him. He had a suitcase full.

AUTHOR: What did you talk about on your trips?

WELBORN: Everything but baseball. Maybe a time or two he told me of something that happened, but nothing of any value. I introduced him to Johnny Mize [the Baseball Hall of Famer from nearby Demorest, Georgia]. They sat down on the ledge of a window, my station for I guess for two hours. Johnny came down there just to see him. I told him Ty was down there just about every day.

[While in California, Welborn met Cobb's two children, Jimmy Cobb and Shirley Beckworth, and their families, and also Cobb's ex-wife, Charlie, who was living with the Beckworths.]

Shirley was married to Dixie Beckworth. Her husband was from Jesup, Georgia. Dixie had an exterminating business, and he had three or four crews. It was a small operation. Long about that time, they had this TV thing on, *Have Gun Will Travel*. Dixie had "Have Flashlight Will Travel," on his calling cards. Cobb's house was only five miles from Shirley's. Ty wouldn't start circulating until about five o'clock in the afternoon, and Dixie would come over to see about us, and then we'd just ride about everywhere. When Dixie came by, he and I would go by his house to see Charlie. She was short and stout, joking and laughing all the time.

AUTHOR: Did Ty ever talk about Charlie?

WELBORN: Never. I don't know that he ever mentioned her to me.

AUTHOR: But Charlie was a real warm person?

WELBORN: Oh, very nice. I don't remember him ever mentioning her. . . . Ty wouldn't go over to Shirley's house where she [Charlie] lived. He would go to the bookstore Shirley had in Palo Alto to see her. It's called Shirley's Bookstore. I have a book that Shirley gave me.

Ty's son, James [Jimmy], brought his family up to visit while I was there. I believe he had three children and his wife was pregnant. They drove up from San Diego in a station wagon. I think they stayed with Beverly next door at night. I believe they had four small children.

AUTHOR: Did you ever meet his second wife, Frances?

WELBORN: Yes, I met her in Mount Airy. I don't know if Ty told me or who told me but she was supposed to have been a relative of the Ballantine Ale people. Somebody told me she was supposed to have more money than Ty. So, she didn't have to put up with any foolishness. She put up with him for as long as she could and she left.

AUTHOR: Did he talk much about his brother, Paul?

WELBORN: I never heard of him. This is the first I've heard of a brother. I never heard that.

(Welborn showed this author and Corley a baseball autographed by Cobb that he had obtained during his California trip.)

He and a doctor friend of his, Dr. Brown from Royston, went to Rome for the Olympics. This was '54 or so, I'm not sure. They came back by Baltimore where they saw the World Series. The players gave Ty this ball. It was on a little lamp, and this part [showing where the stand would be] was a baseball bat. It had a shade on it and this ball was sticking right on top. I saw it sitting in a corner there at his home, and I asked him, "Ty, who gave you this?" and he said, "Hell, I don't know, but I'll give it to you," and he pulled the ball's cover off it, and just wadded the thing up—he'd been drinking—and he threw it in a corner. I said, "As long as you got it off, autograph it for me," and that's how come his autograph is on that ball.

AUTHOR: Did he ever get remorseful near the end and say there were some things he would have done different?

WELBORN: No, it looked like he was glad what he did all the way through.

# Sources

## Books

*Augusta: A Pictorial History,* by Helen Callahan, Donning (1980)

*Augusta: A Postcard History,* by Joseph M. Lee III,
Arcadia Publishing (1997)

*The Augusta Chronicle: Indomitable Voice of Dixie, 1785–1960,*
by Earl Bell and Kenneth Crabbe, University of Georgia Press (1960)

Augusta City Directories

*Baseball's Greatest Managers,* by Edwin Pope,
Doubleday & Company (1960)

*The Biographical Encyclopedia of the Negro Baseball Leagues,*
James A. Riley, editor, Carroll & Graf (2002)

*Complete Book of Baseball's Negro Leagues,* by John B. Holway,
Hastings House (2001)

*The Encyclopedia of the South,* Robert O'Brien, editor, with
Harold H. Martin, Facts On File Publications (1985)

*Georgia: The WPA Guide to Its Towns and Countryside,* compiled by workers of the Writer's Program of the Works Progress Administration in the state of Georgia, University of South Carolina Press (1940, reprint 1990)

*Great Georgians,* by Zell Miller, Advocate Press (1983)

*Historical Markers and Monuments of Richmond County, Georgia,* by Marguerite Flint Fogleman, Richmond County Historical Society (1986)

*The Letters of Archie Butt, Personal Aide to President Roosevelt,* by Archibald Willingham Butt, edited with a biographical sketch of the author by Lawrence F. Abbott, Kessinger Publishing (originally published 1924, new version 2005)

*My Life in Baseball: The True Record,* by Ty Cobb, with Al Stump, Amereon House (1961)

*Peach: Ty Cobb in His Time and Ours,* by Richard Bak, Sports Media Group (2005)

*The Story of Augusta,* by Edward J. Cashin, Richmond County Board of Education (1980)

*The Story of Ty Cobb: Baseball's Greatest Player,* by Gene Schoor, Julian Messner (1952)

*They Shaped the Game: Ty Cobb, Babe Ruth, and Jackie Robinson,* by William Jay Jacobs, Atheneum (1994)

*Ty Cobb,* by Charles C. Alexander, Oxford University Press (1984)

*Ty Cobb: His Tumultuous Life and Times,* by Richard Bak, Taylor Publishers (1994)

*Ty Cobb: A Biography,* by Dan Holmes, Baseball's All-Time Greatest Hitters series, Greenwood Press (2004)

*Ty Cobb,* by Norman L. Macht, Baseball Legends series (1995)

*Ty Cobb,* by Dennis Abrams, Baseball Superstars series, Chelsea House Publications (2007)

*Ty Cobb,* by John Dennis McCallum, Henry Holt & Co (1975)

*Ty Cobb: The Greatest,* by Robert Rubin, Putnam (1978)

*The Ty Cobb Scrapbook: An Illustrated Chronology of Significant Dates in the 24-Year Career of the Fabled Georgia Peach—Over 800 Games From 1905–1928,* by Marc Okkonen, Sterling (2002)

*Tyrus,* by Patrick Creevy, Forge Books (2002)

## NEWSPAPERS

*Athens (GA) Daily News*
*Atlanta (GA) Constitution*
*Augusta (GA) Chronicle*
*Augusta (GA) Herald*
*New York Times*
*News Leader* (Royston, GA)
*USA Today*

## MAGAZINES

*Athens Magazine*
*Augusta* (magazine)
*Banks County Lifestyle Magazine*
*The Baseball Magazine*

## SPECIAL PLACES

*Augusta Genealogical Society Adamson Library,* 1109 Broad Street, Augusta, GA 30901, (706) 722-4073, augustagensociety.org

*Augusta Museum of History,* 560 Reynolds Street, Augusta, GA 30901, (706) 722-8454, augustamuseum.org

*Augusta-Richmond County Historical Society,* Reese Library, Augusta State University, Augusta, GA 30904, (706) 737-1532, thearchs.org

*East Central Georgia Regional Library* (Georgia special collections), 902 Greene Street, Augusta, GA 30901, (706) 821-2600, ecgrl.public.lib.ga.us/rco.htm

*Exchange Club of Augusta Fairgrounds* (formerly Warren Park baseball field), Third and Hale Streets, Augusta, GA

*Georgia Sports Hall of Fame,* 301 Cherry Street, Macon, GA 31208, (478) 752-1585, gshf.org

*Louisville Slugger Museum and Factory,* 800 West Main Street, Louisville, KY 40202, (877) 775-8443, sluggermuseum.org (order your own personalized bat)

*Magnolia Cemetery,* 702 Third Street, Augusta, GA 30901, (706) 821-1746, www.augustaga.gov (where Cobb's former in-laws and friends are buried)

*The Narrows community,* Georgia Highway 105 (Ty Cobb Parkway) just southeast of Cornelia, Georgia (where Cobb was born)

*National Baseball Hall of Fame and Museum,* 25 Main Street, Cooperstown, NY 13326, (607) 547-7200, toll free: (888) 425-5633, baseballhalloffame.org

*Negro Leagues Baseball Museum,* 1616 East 18th Street, Kansas City, MO 64108, (816) 221-1920, (888) 221-NLBM, nlb.com

*Rose Hill Cemetery,* off Georgia Highway 17 South, Royston, Georgia (where Cobb is entombed in a mausoleum)

*Steak House,* 1735 Willingham Avenue, Cornelia, GA 30531, (706) 778-4351 (Cobb photos)

*Ty Cobb Museum,* 461 Cook Street, Royston, GA 30662, (706) 245-1825, tycobbmuseum.org

## WEB SOURCES

About North Georgia: http://ngeorgia.com/people
Amazon.com: www.amazon.com
Arcadia Publishing: www.arcadiapublishing.com
Augusta Chronicle archives: www.augustaarchives.com
Augusta Chronicle: http://augustachronicle.com
Augusta GreenJackets: www.greenjacketsbaseball.com
Baseball Almanac: www.baseball-almanac.com
Baseball Fever: http://baseball-fever.com/archive
Baseball Guru: www.baseballguru.com
Baseball Library: www.baseballlibrary.com
The Baseball Page: www.thebaseballpage.com
Baseball references: www.baseball-reference.com
Baseball Savvy: www.baseballsavvy.com
Detroit Public Library: www.detroitpubliclibrary.org
Detroit Tigers: http://detroit.tigers.mlb.com
Free Library of Philadelphia: www.library.phila.gov
The Globe Pequot Press: www.globepequot.com
Internet Movie Database: www.imdb.com
John Skilton's Baseball Links: www.baseball-links.com
Library of Congress: www.loc.gov
Louisville Slugger Museum & Factory: www.sluggermuseum.org
Major League Baseball: www.mlb.com
Minor League Baseball: web.minorleaguebaseball.com
National Baseball Hall of Fame & Museum: web.baseballhalloffame.org
Negro Baseball Leagues: www.blackbaseball.com
Negro League Baseball: www.negroleaguebaseball.com
Negro Leagues Baseball Museum: www.nlbm.com
Official Ty Cobb Web site: www.cmgww.com/baseball/cobb
Philadelphia Athletics Historical Society: www.philadelphiaathletics.org
South Atlantic League: www.southatlanticleague.com
Sporting News: www.sportingnews.com

Ty Cobb Educational Foundation: www.tycobbfoundation.com
Ty Cobb: The Home Page: http://wso.williams.edu/~jkossuth/cobb
Ty Cobb Museum: www.tycobbmuseum.org
Wikipedia: www.wikipedia.org

# INDEX

# ABOUT THE AUTHOR

DON RHODES is publications editor of Morris Communications Co. based in Augusta, Georgia. He is also known for *Ramblin' Rhodes,* the longest running country music column in America, now in its thirty-seventh year. His articles have appeared in many daily newspapers and national magazines, and he has been nominated several times to the Georgia Music Hall of Fame in the non-performer category. Don lives in North Augusta, South Carolina.